The Ultimate 365 Day Activity Book for Couples

D1569256

Dreamstorm Publications

A Gift for You

Most of the material I write about is centered on developing our inner selves. Thus, as you might've guessed, my readers are usually introverts. I can appreciate that because I'm an introvert myself. However, as an introvert, I'm also aware of our social shortcomings. This is why I have decided to gift you with some amazing material for your growth. By simply clicking the link below, you will have access to the *Introvert Survival Kit* and *Inward Thrive* Email Series for free.

Visit the following site or click here for full access: http://bit.ly/introvertsk

This powerful bundle will help you make massive improvements in your social life. It contains 3 Ebooks and 2 articles:

- EBook 1: Making and Keeping Friends: Developing Friendships that Last a Lifetime in this Fast Paced World!
- EBook 2: How to Stop Worrying and Start Living Effectively In the 21st Century: An Updated Guide to Living Free of Worry in the Knowledge Era
- EBook 3: High Impact Communication: Tips on Getting Your Strongest Message Across in 1 Minute
- Article 1: How to Break the Cycle of Anxiety and Enjoy Social Situations
- Article 2: Be an Introvert and Have an Active Social Life

Along with the material, you will also get a lot of bonus gifts in the days to come. I'd recommend not missing out! Just go to http://bit.ly/introvertsk

I also have a special invitation for those appreciate a good read. If you'd like to be part of the review process of many of our upcoming books (and receive free copies!) and click here: http://bit.ly/itadvancedreview I will send you details of what it entails through mail. Thanks!

Introduction

Love is a wonderful adventure, until it's not. That's where this book comes in. We can all agree that at the peak of a blossoming relationship, you have two human beings deeply in love with each other and willing to go any lengths to bring joy to the other. It's a wonderful feeling that has no equal. Yet, inevitably time and the unyielding pressures of life turn this wonderful experience to something casual- an everyday activity. Time spent as a couple goes from being a dream-like experience to part of the daily grind. Some call it inevitable, stating that it's a phase every relationship goes through. Is this really the case?

Careful studies of thriving couples say otherwise.

You see, a great relationship is constantly fed, kind of like a campfire. Both parties constantly contribute to growing this flame of passion, love, and understanding. Great couples understand this and practice this by engaging in activities that renew the sense of spontaneity and surprise we all love. This is what this book is all about.

In the pages to come you will find exciting prompts, ideas and questions that will allow both of you to discover more about yourselves, look into who you are as a couple, have tons of fun, and write out adventures to your heart's content.

Enjoy!

Why and How You Should Journal with Your Loved One

Apart from journaling being a wonderful way to vent out emotions, spark creativity, and improve penmanship, it's also an amazing way to grow a bond with a loved one.

- **A journal gives a couple something to work towards and focus on.** Some prompts, e.g.., will help couples gain a sense of direction as to where they are in their relationship. Others will reveal parts of your personality you didn't know you had.

- **A journal helps creating lifelong memories as a couple.** Memories are easily among the best things in life, especially if they're created with a loved one by your side. Who knows? Maybe both of you will end up having children or even grandchildren (no pressure if you don't have any already). For sure you'll love to have a book filled with the things you both experienced and accomplished to share with them.

- **A journal will help both become more productive in achieving those #relationshipsgoals.** As you progress through the journal and start thinking up your own date ideas or bucket list, you'll have clarity as to the things you'll want to do as a couple. Clarity of intent is the mother of all productivity.

- **Enhances your drive in reaching your goals.** A journal can be a powerful tool for self-discovery. Getting to know someone is a lifelong process, however, we can all agree that certain activities, when performed as a couple, can help speed up this process. When a couple engages in a journaling activity, they begin unraveling more of their personalities, personal philosophies and outlooks on life. Weaknesses and strengths will become more apparent and growing acceptance of these qualities in one another will be inevitable.

We invite you not only to begin this journal but to make journaling in general part of your life. It's an experience that will grow on you , we promise. Together, we will help you and your significant other come up with ideas, inspire dreams, discover yourselves and the world around you both.

Are you ready to take your relationship to the next level?

365 Days of Fun Date Ideas, Self-Discovery Questions, and Creative Writing Prompts for Couples

Day 1 ☼ Date Idea   /   /

A Jigsaw Puzzle

One of the most frustrating games for sure, but it will train the both of you to stretch your patience a bit more!

His take on the date idea...   **Her take on the date idea...**

Day 2 ☼ Wanderlust   /   /

Where on Earth have you been dying to visit?

Both will list 5 destinations that you really want to visit. The challenge is agreeing on one as your next vacation destination.

His Answer...   **Her Answer...**

"We love because it's the only true adventure."

-Nikki Giovanni

Day 3 ☼ Aspirations / /

As children, what did both of you want to be when you grew up?

Children have no limits in their thinking. This is why this is a great starting point for figuring out if you've both maintained (or evolved) your passions to date.

His Answer...   **Her Answer...**

Day 4 ☼ Making Connections / /

Make a list of people you don't know personally but would love to meet.

Making this list could end up in an unexpected visit or email. Perhaps it could even define your next adventure together.

His Answer...   **Her Answer...**

"It was love at first sight, at last sight, at ever and ever sight."

-Vladimir Nabokov

Day 5 ☼ Four Seasons   /   /

Which would prefer? Winter, spring, summer or fall?

Is cold and white snow your thing? Or is it the warmth of the desert?

His Answer…   **Her Answer…**

Day 6 ☼ Being a Multi Lingual   /   /

Are you interested in learning a foreign language?

Learning something together can strengthen your bond as a couple. If given a chance, what language would you like to learn and why are you interested in it?

His Answer…   **Her Answer…**

"Every love story is beautiful, but ours is my favorite."

-Unknown

Day 7 ☼ Photo Prompt   /   /

Go through your photo album; what particular photo shows one of the happiest moments in your relationship? Tell the story behind it.

"We accept the love we think we deserve."

-Stephen Chbosky

Eternal love

One day at work, Amanda received a beautiful flower bouquet. In it, she counted 11 flowers and found a short note in it. It was written in beautiful lettering and said:

"My love for you will last until the day the last flower in this bouquet dies."

The note was from her husband who had gone on a business trip. Unsure as to what to make of the message, she went home in the evening and soaked the flowers with water. One day after another, the flowers became a little less beautiful until they all died. All but one flower. This was the day when she realized that there was one artificial flower in the bouquet that would last forever.

"Love harder than any pain you've ever felt."
-Unknown

Day 8 ☼ Date Idea /   /

Coffee Date

Alright, so this is the most basic date ever. But you'll get to catch up with each other without feeling dizzy or puking on the side of the table.

His take on the date idea...   **Her take on the date idea...**

Day 9 ☼ Food for Love /   /

What are your favorite foods? Do you find it quite fun to dig into spicy food, or the other one just doesn't like it?

There are places best known for their specialty dishes. What is your favorite restaurant? Are you the type of couple who enjoys the gastronomic adventure together?

His Answer...   **Her Answer...**

"If I know what love is, it is because of you."

-Hermann Hesse

Day 10 ☼ Dream Talent   /   /

Is there anything you would like to learn since you were a child?

Perhaps, you'll discover something new about each other by discussing the things you really fancy doing since you were a little kid. Was there a particular skill you wish you had? With enough support from your partner, are you still willing to try it?

His Answer...   **Her Answer...**

Day 11 ☼ One Moment   /   /

What is one special occasion that you want to celebrate together?

Celebrating special events with your partner allows you to make more memories as a couple. In what particular occasion do you spend more time together and why is it important?

His Answer...   **Her Answer...**

"Love loves to love love."

-James Joyce

Day 12 ☼ Unwanted Fears   /   /

If fear isn't an obstacle, what challenge are you willing to go through?

An exciting relationship is something that encourages you to face your fears rather than succumb to them. What is one thing that you wish to try – individually or together – granting that you have enough courage to do so?

His Answer...   **Her Answer...**

Day 13 ☼ Feeling Uncomfortable   /   /

What usually hinders you from being fully open to someone?

As much as we'd like to be completely honest with our partners, we sometimes feel judged even before opening up to them. What is one thing you wish your partner could change in order for you to be more comfortable in sharing what you really feel?

His Answer...   **Her Answer...**

"When love is not madness, it is not love."

-Pedro Calderon de la Barca

Day 14 ☼ Photo Prompt

Show us your first picture together. What is the difference between that and the latest one? How did your relationship change or improve since the first picture was taken?

"Love is friendship set on fire."

-Jeremy Taylor

Don't Wait

When he arrived at her door unexpectedly, the first thing he said was,

"I shouldn't have come."

Her kiss told him he was wrong.

He should have come years ago.

"I love you. I am at rest with you. I have come home."

-Dorothy L. Sayers

Day 15 ☼ Date Idea   /   /

Fruit-picking Date

Then prepare some fresh fruit shakes after! Ah, what a healthy way to spend your time together!

His take on the date idea...   **Her take on the date idea...**

Day 16 ☼ Positivity   /   /

How do you keep your relationship away from negativity?

Being surrounded by good-natured people and circumstances is the key to leading a peaceful life. How do you maintain the positive vibes in your relationship?

His Answer...   **Her Answer...**

"I have found that if you love life, life will love you back."

-Arthur Rubinstein

Day 17 ☼ Wishes / /

If a genie appears and tells you he would grant you 3 wishes, what would those wishes be?

This question is just for fun, but it could help you recognize your partner's unusual wishes or desires. Would you request for material things or intangible pleasure such as happiness and contentment?

His Answer...   **Her Answer...**

Day 18 ☼ Life Lesson / /

What life lesson would you probably tell your grandchildren in the future?
As years pass by, you face different trials as a couple and – with enough love and trust – overcome them together. What particular life lesson do you think your future grandchildren should learn about?

His Answer...   **Her Answer...**

"Love is when you meet someone who tells you something new about yourself."
-Andre Breton

Day 19 ☼ Family   /   /

How many kids would you like to have?

Some couples are not comfortable having this kind of conversation, particularly when they are in the early stage of their relationship. But if the time is finally right, what kind of family do you wish to build? Do you like a just a small one, or do you believe that more is actually merrier?

His Answer...   **Her Answer...**

Day 20 ☼ Dream Vacation   /   /

If you have an entire week to spend on vacation, how exactly would you like to spend it?

Working on your future together is definitely good. Nevertheless, you have to take some time off to relax and refresh your whole being. What kind of activities would you like to do to reinvigorate yourself?

His Answer...   **Her Answer...**

"Love is never wrong."

-Melissa Etheridge

Day 21 ☼ Photo Prompt

Choose your favorite solo photo of your partner. Why was it your favorite? Does he/she look dazzling in that shot, or was there a particular story behind it?

"We love the things we love for what they are."

-Robert Frost

Love You Won't Forget

A guy meets a girl. They date for a year and for some reason the guy breaks-up with her.

One fine day, they bump into each other on the street.

Guy: Hi, you look prettier than before.

Girl: Many people think I'm beautiful.

Guy: Yes, I know that. You're pretty, very kind and wonderful. Who's the lucky guy?

Girl: I'm single.

Guy: Why? Don't you want to be in a relationship?

Girl: Yes, I do.

Guy: So, what's the problem? Don't tell me no one loves you?

Girl: A few guys do.

Guy: Are they bad?

Girl: No, they're fine. They're very sweet.

Guy: Then what's the problem?

Girl: It's you. I can't stop loving you.

The few seconds of silence that followed seemed like an eternity.

Finally, the guy whispered back

"Me too."

"Do you have a reason for loving?"

-Bridgett Bardot

Day 22 ☼ Date Idea   /   /

Spa Date

If you are both busy at work and have to give up some of your quality time, then a massage date should be fun and relax at the same time. This will reinvigorate your whole being and will help you become more efficient at work – and at home with your loved one.

His take on the date idea...   **Her take on the date idea...**

Day 23 ☼ Luxurious Surprise   /   /

If money was not an issue, what expensive gift would you like to give your partner?

Both will list 5 destinations that you really want to visit. The challenge is agreeing on one as your next vacation destination.

His Answer...   **Her Answer...**

"A flower cannot blossom without sunshine, and man cannot live without love."

-Max Muller

Day 24 ☼ Inspire Others   /   /

In a class reunion, what are the things that you will openly share?

Comparing each one's achievement, unfortunately, really happens during get-togethers. It makes a lot of people uncomfortable, particularly those who had it rough. What are the things you've accomplished as a couple that you would willingly share?

His Answer...   **Her Answer...**

Day 25 ☼ Time Machine   /   /

If you have the power to do things over again, what will you change in your life?

We all have our fair share of bad decisions, and some of these haunt us for a long time. What will you change if you ever get the chance?

His Answer...   **Her Answer...**

"Being in love with you makes every day an interesting one."

-Unknown

Day 26 ☼ Big No   /   /

5 traits you usually dislike.

Acknowledging behaviors that we do not like is a step to learning more about ourselves. List down 5 behaviors you despise and reasons why you think people should change them.

His Answer...   Her Answer...

Day 27 ☼ My Savior   /   /

Who do you consider your life hero?

We all have that (childhood) hero in the form of our grandmother, favorite teacher or best friend. Tell us more about this person. What did this person do for you to look up to him/her?

His Answer...   Her Answer...

"I love you a lottle, its like a little but a lot."

-Unknown

Day 28 ☼ Photo Prompt

Choose a photo that you think was the funniest. Reminisce the time when you were both having fun doing something silly. Why are moments like this very precious?

"The giving of love is an education in itself."

-Eleanor Roosevelt

Thank You for Being You

You are such a gift to me. Having you in my life is such a blessing.

Every day, I thank God that you are in my life and that you are by my side.

I am so blessed to be able to call you mine and to be called yours.

I pray that I will always be able to give you what you need in life

and that you will always be there to hold my hand

and that you will continue to walk with me on this journey that we call life.

"Speak low, if you speak love."

-William Shakespeare

Day 29 ☼ Date Idea / /

Kite-flying Date

Seriously, when was the last time you ever flew a kite? In fact, have you ever tried once? This activity takes a lot of patience, and you may enjoy how it feels like to be little kids once again.

His take on the date idea...

Her take on the date idea...

Day 30 ☼ Motivation / /

How do you motivate each other to persevere at work?

Maintaining productivity and possibly stepping up the career ladder are no easy feat. You cheer each other up and find reasons to carry on. When the other one is getting burnt out, what do you do to uplift his/her spirit?

His Answer...

Her Answer...

"If you love it enough, anything will talk with you."

-George Washington Carver

Day 31 ☼ Inspiration   /   /

If you were given a chance to meet someone famous or prominent in his field, who will it be?

Discuss this with your partner. Let's say, the two of you can only choose ONE. Who would you like to meet and what are the factors you consider in choosing this person?

His Answer...   **Her Answer...**

Day 32 ☼ Wild Dreams   /   /

What runs into your head when you're awake in bed late at night?

Do you play different life scenarios in your mind, or imagine yourself in a totally different situation? Where are your midnight thoughts taking you?

His Answer...   **Her Answer...**

"If a thing loves, it is infinite."

-William Blake

Day 33 ☼ Apple of the Eye   1 / 4 / 2021

How can someone get your attention?

List down 5 things that a person can do to successfully catch your interest; it could
be something you like or something you hate. How do you react when you notice
that someone is deliberately trying to get your attention?

His Answer...
- Say something funny
- Wear something flashy.
- Put on a song I like
- Know an interesting fact.
- Bite my hand

I usually ignore people who deliberately try to get my attention.

Her Answer...
- Have good music taste
- Be smart
- Be artsy
- Be active/adventurous
- Be funny

It depends if I like them

Day 34 ☼ Sensitivity   / /

**What, for you, is the most insensitive thing a person can do that may hurt your
feelings?**

Whether or not you are in a relationship, it is always good to consider other
people's feelings, especially if you are about to drop a sensitive comment. How do
you handle insensitive actions? Do you usually keep it to yourself, or do you let
the other person know about it?

His Answer...

Her Answer...

"Love comforteth like sunshine after rain."

-William Shakespeare

Day 35 ☼ Photo Prompt   /   /

Pick a photo of you (or together) that you hate. Why do think this photo is embarrassing? Your partner may actually find it hilarious so for the sake of sharing, go show it!

"Love is a game that two can play and both win."

-Eva Gabor

Dreams Come True

She dreamed of a love so great it surrounded her with constant warmth and transformed

her into stronger and more beautiful woman than she was without it.

When she awoke and felt her wife's body snuggled up next to her

she knew it wasn't just a dream.

"Loving you never was an option – it was necessity."

-Unknown

Day 36 ☼ Date Idea   /   /

Workout Together

Whether you are both health buff or not, working out together once in awhile is always a good idea. Once you started to entertain the thought of giving up, you'll always have your partner to cheer you up.

His take on the date idea...   **Her take on the date idea...**

Day 37 ☼ Life Lessons   /   /

List down 5 important things in life that you've learned from random people.
We get to learn valuable life lessons from family and friends, but sometimes, we meet "temporary people" who share with us their inspiring or thought-provoking experiences. What are the 5 life-relevant lessons have you acquired from these people that you find true or useful?

His Answer...   **Her Answer...**

"A man is already halfway in love with any woman who listens to him."

-Brendan Francis

Day 38 ☼ Talents   /   /

As List down 5 new skills that you want to learn.

Being a skillful person helps us accomplish a lot of things, and may even be a reason for younger people to land a good job in the future. What are the 5 useful skills you wish to acquire and why do you think they are relevant to your life?

His Answer...   **Her Answer...**

Day 39 ☼ Biggest Decision   /   /

What is the biggest life decision – individually and as a couple – you've made?

How did this decision change your life up to this day? What are the things you consider before coming up with this resolution?

His Answer...   **Her Answer...**

"Your love is all I need to feel complete."

-Unknown

Day 40 ☼ Making Routines   /   /

What are the simple things that make your life easier on a daily basis?

List down 3 to 5 simple things in your home that actually make life easier for you; it could be the microwave you always use to reheat your food when you're in a hurry. Simply anything you find necessary no matter how small it is.

His Answer...   **Her Answer...**

Day 41 ☼ Priorities   /   /

What job would you never do no matter how good the pay is?

Some people choose practicality over comfort, while some are willing to take their time in finding the job that would best suit their personality. Try to expand as to why you are not willing to take this particular job despite the good salary offer.

His Answer...   **Her Answer...**

"There is more pleasure in loving than in being beloved."

-Thomas Fuller

Day 42 ☼ Photo Prompt

Pick a childhood photo of your partner that you really like. What can you say about his/her younger image? Do you think you could have been good friends if you met each other that time?

"If music be the food of love, play on."

-William Shakespeare

When It's Time to Apologize and Start Anew

The only word that I can say is that I'm sorry,

I've cried so much, but please don't worry.

I need you more every growing day,

But sorry is what I feel to say.

I admit that I've been out of line,

But I promise you that I'm going to re-align.

My insecurity is going to drive us apart,

But I will never let what's special depart.

My hand in yours is its belonging,

But this hurt shall not keep prolonging.

Please keep my heart safe and warm,

We shall get past this brief storm.

"Stand by your man. Give him two arms to cling to and something warm to come to."

-Tammy Wynette

Day 43 ☼ Date Idea   /   /

Cook Dinner Together

It has been said that the best way to a man's heart is through his stomach. But why not do the cooking together if it's actually fun?

His take on the date idea...   **Her take on the date idea...**

Day 44 ☼ Stressors   /   /

List down 5 things that cause you stress.

Some things are beyond our control; be it at work, school or home, there are stressful circumstances that we cannot really avoid. What are the things that stress you out?

His Answer...   **Her Answer...**

"Wherever you are and whatever you do, be in love."

-Rumi

Day 45 ☼ Stress Relievers   /   /

(Continuation of Day 44)

But most importantly, how do you try to deal with your stress? Do you have any particular activity that helps you relax? Do you prefer relieving your stress alone, or with your partner?

His Answer...   **Her Answer...**

Day 46 ☼ Creepiest Fears   /   /

What animal/insect do you fear the most?

Isn't it cute to find out that your partner panics more than you do whenever he sees an insect flying towards him (and vice versa)?

His Answer...   **Her Answer...**

"Love all, trust a few, do wrong to none."

-William Shakespeare

Day 47 ☼ Confusions   /   /

What is the most confusing situation you've been in?

We all go through a confusing phase at some point in our lives. How did you try to overcome this period?

His Answer...   **Her Answer...**

Day 48 ☼ Phobia   /   /

Do you have any serious phobia?

When our phobia is triggered by natural circumstance, it could hinder us from enjoying a lot of adventurous activities. Are your actions limited by certain phobias? How does it affect your life in general? Do you try to overcome this fear, or you just learned to live with it?

His Answer...   **Her Answer...**

"Time doesn't matter love is forever."

-Unknown

Day 49 ☼ Photo Prompt   /   /

Show your partner a photo of you with your childhood friends. Share with him/her one childhood story with these kids that you'll never forget.

"Unable are the loved to die, for love is immortality."

-Emily Dickinson

What is Love

Love decides everything in this world. It doesn't have any conditions or boundaries.
We don't know exactly what love is and where it comes from.

But one thing is sure: we are nothing without love!
There are times when we feel shy and timid, when we are afraid of expressing the love
we feel. Being afraid of embarrassing the other person or ourselves we hesitate to say the
actual words "I love you".

One can say "I love you" in many ways: by means of nice presents and little notes, s
miles and sometimes tears.

"Love is a better master than duty."
-Albert Einstein

Day 50 ☼ Date Idea   /   /

Go Get Drunk!

Alright, I know we just agreed how handy it is not to puke in public places. But really, have you tried getting drunk together? Like the naughty-level kind of drunk? Alcohol-induced sex is still one of the bests.

His take on the date idea...   **Her take on the date idea...**

Day 51 ☼ Happy Thoughts   /   /

List down 5 simple things that can make you smile.

Appreciating every little thing that surrounds us, right from the moment we wake up, is a simple way of living a happy life. What are the little things that can make you smile?

His Answer...   **Her Answer...**

"What is love? It is the morning and the evening star."

-Sinclair Lewis

Day 52 ☼ Golden Memories   /   /

Describe your childhood.

Childhood is a big part of who we are; it has shaped us to become the person that we are today. Tell us about your childhood and share why it is one of your fondest memories in life.

His Answer...   **Her Answer...**

Day 53 ☼ Role Model   /   /

Who has the greatest influence in your life?

Your partner may be thankful for your good traits, but there is someone else responsible for that; someone who has made a great impact in your life and later became a great influence in everything you do. Who is that person and in what way did he/she change your perspectives?

His Answer...   **Her Answer...**

" 'Tis better to have loved and lost, than never to have loved at all."

-Alfred Tennyson

Day 54 ☼ Frustrations   /   /

Individually and as a couple, what is your biggest regret?

Perhaps it was the time you had to chance to travel abroad together but didn't push through. Or that time when you were offered a good position in the company but got scared of the overwhelming responsibilities so you declined. What was your biggest regret as an individual and as a couple?

His Answer...   **Her Answer...**

Day 55 ☼ Understanding   /   /

How responsible are you from each other's perspective?

This is a very deliberate question and requires an enormous amount of understanding as a mature couple. Do you find your partner responsible enough, or do you think he/she needs a little push?

His Answer...   **Her Answer...**

"First love is only a little foolishness and a lot of curiosity."

-George Bernard Shaw

Day 56 ☼ Photo Prompt

Pick a photo where you feel really confident of yourself. Tell us why you felt that way.

"Love's gift cannot be given, it waits to be accepted."

-Rabindranath Tagore

Our First Kiss

At last they kissed. Although they both had desperately wanted to all evening,

when it finally happened it was not so much out of boldness but, rather,

because neither of them could think of anything else to say.

"Genuine love involves not only passion, but also commitment and wisdom."

-Unknown

Day 57 ☼ Date Idea   /   /

Travel Together

This is a common #relationshipgoal but visiting a place you haven't been before, at least once in awhile, will allow you to create more wonderful memories together.

His take on the date idea...   **Her take on the date idea...**

Day 58 ☼ Being Proud   /   /

What is one thing your partner did, or a trait he possesses, that makes you really proud?

It could be the time he helped someone in need or the fact that he is really smart. What exactly makes you a proud partner?

His Answer...   **Her Answer...**

"When love is at its best, one loves so much that he cannot forget."

-Helen Hunt Jackson

Day 59 ☼ The Best Teacher   /   /

Is there something life has recently taught you?

Be it a good or bad realization, life hits us hard with new lessons every now and then. Have you had any light-bulb moment recently?

His Answer...   **Her Answer...**

Day 60 ☼ The Best Day   /   /

What is your definition of an ideal day?

Away from work, of course; but aside from this, what else can make your day perfect?

His Answer...   **Her Answer...**

"It is the time you have wasted for your rose that makes your rose so important."

-Antoine de Saint-Exupéry

Day 61 ☼ Delays   /   /

List down 3 or more things that distract you from getting your work done.

Try to write down as many things as you can; the goal is to identify whatever it is that hinders you from finishing up your task. This could lead to a realization – perhaps you can come up with a resolution on how to avoid the following distractions next time.

His Answer...   **Her Answer...**

Day 62 ☼ Golden Years   /   /

City or countryside, which do you prefer more?

If not everyone, at least most of us dream of settling down someday. Where do you imagine spending the later years of your life, and what kind of lifestyle do you wish to enjoy by then?

His Answer...   **Her Answer...**

"Love is a trap. When it appears, we see only its light, not its shadows."

-Paulo Coehlo

Day 63 ☼ Photo Prompt

Show us a photo of you two taken during a formal event. We may not always see our partners dressed in a formal suit or gown, so how dazzling do you think he/she was?

"Love is an energy which exists of itself. It is its own value."

-Thornton Wilder

Love is Blind

She was a beautiful girl, with a beautiful family, and a beautiful boyfriend. The only problem was that she was blind. She felt deeply insecure and hated herself for it.

One day, they got news from the health department that someone had agreed to donate their eyes to her. The girl was elated! After so many years, she would see again! Immediately, she started making plans to marry her beloved. Her boyfriend just smiled and hugged her. The day arrived, and the operation was a success. When she opened her eyes and called for her boyfriend, she found out he had left. She was heartbroken.

Time passed, and her boyfriend returned to her. He had lost his sight. He worked up the courage to try to reignite the relationship and eventually proposed to her. She thought of the burden being with a blind person would be and declined his offer. As they said their goodbyes, he looked down, brokenhearted, and mumbled, "Take care of yourself... and of my eyes". He left, and she never knew of him again.

Though she didn't understand it at first, she later found out that her ex had been her donor. Thanks to him, she got her life back and could see the world. She chose to do what was right and spent the rest of her life looking for the man that gave her back her life.

"Loving you is both my biggest weakness and greatest strength."
-Unknown

Day 64 ☼ Date Idea   /   /

Shop Together

Okay, you don't necessarily have to spend a lot. But perhaps you can buy your partner that sexy lingerie you've always wanted her to try!

His take on the date idea...   **Her take on the date idea...**

Day 65 ☼ Happy Thoughts   /   /

What is your happiest memory as a couple?

The longer you've been together, the more memories you make. What is the fondest memory you can think of with your partner, and why was this moment special?

His Answer...   **Her Answer...**

"Eternity is in love with the productions of time."

-William Blake

Day 66 ☼ Achievements / /

What is your greatest accomplishment together?

It could be the time you finally moved into your own place or the time you were both promoted at work. What is the greatest relationship accomplishment you've reached so far?

His Answer...   **Her Answer...**

Day 67 ☼ Significant Support / /

Write down 3 to 5 ways you support each other.

Relationship means teamwork; it becomes more successful when the two people involved always have each other's back. In what way do you support one another?

His Answer...   **Her Answer...**

"If thou must love me, let it be for naught except for love's sake only."

-Elizabeth Barrett Browning

Day 68 ☼ Mannerisms   /   /

Is there anything that your partner does which makes you uncomfortable?

Does your partner have a certain mannerism or attitude issues that make you feel really awkward? Are you willing to let him/her know about this?

His Answer...   **Her Answer...**

Day 69 ☼ Being Patient   /   /

Create your own list of the things that are worth waiting for.

It could be having a family, or finally stepping up that career ladder. Ponder on the prompt and write down the things you think are worth stretching your patience for.

His Answer...   **Her Answer...**

"The spaces between your fingers are meant to be filled with mine."

-Unknown

Day 70 ☼ Photo Prompt

Show your favorite class picture to your partner and share one of your fondest
memories as a student.

"You don't have to promise me the moon or stars...
just promise that you will stand under them with me."

-Unknown

Love At First Laugh

When the joke ended, the room was painfully silent

except for a snortle from a blonde near the back of the room.

In that moment he realized that what he wanted more than a future in comedy

was a future with her.

"I'm much more me when I'm with you."

-Unknown

Day 71 ☼ Date Idea   /   /

Volunteer Together

Do you enjoy playing with kids? Or taking care of pets? There are a lot of charity institutions to choose from. Aside from the time, you'll be able to spend together, it can lead you to several life realizations that may help your relationship become stronger.

His take on the date idea...   **Her take on the date idea...**

Day 72 ☼ Approval From Others   /   /

How far would you go just to impress others?

We all try to impress other people for many reasons, and it's actually a good thing because it could mean we're working hard to get what we want. But how far are you willing to go just to get someone's respect and admiration?

His Answer...   **Her Answer...**

"1 universe, 9 planets, 204 countries, 809 islands, 7 seas, and I had the privilege to meet you."

-Unknown

Day 73 ☼ Escapade   /   /

What is your dream adventure as a couple?

Making as many memories will give you something to look back to when you're both old. What is the greatest adventure you wish to do together and why?

His Answer...   **Her Answer...**

Day 74 ☼ Fulfillment   /   /

What do you think are the components of a satisfying life?

What are the things that you wish to have in your life before you can finally say that you have everything you need?

His Answer...   **Her Answer...**

"If a hug represented how much I loved you, I would hold you in my arms forever."

-Mandy Hampton

Day 75 ☼ Life in Songs   /   /

Write down your top 5 most favorite songs.

Is They say music helps us express certain emotions, especially if one does not
have the courage to say what's on his mind. What are the songs that best describe
your feelings towards your partner? Or perhaps, the songs that best describe your
life?

His Answer...   **Her Answer...**

Day 76 ☼ Self-Reliance   /   /

How do you boost your self-confidence?

Being confident helps us get through a lot of trials, be it at work or personal
endeavors. What do you do in order to acquire enough assertiveness?

His Answer...   **Her Answer...**

"I know there are plenty of fish in the sea, but I think you're my Nemo."

-Unknown

Day 77 ☼ Photo Prompt   /   /

Select a random photo from your partner's album. Ask anything you find interesting or intriguing about this photo.

"I knew that I loved you when suddenly 'home' went from a place to a person."

-Unknown

A Well-deserved Prom Night

Alex and his grandmother always had a unique bond with each other.

He would spend hours with her, listening to his grandmother's stories of a lifetime.

She once told him that she had met his grandfather a long time after graduating from high

school. This was also the reason why she was never asked out to go to prom.

When the day of Alex's prom had arrived, his grandmother was so excited for him.

She had watched him save money for months so that he could afford a tuxedo and even a

limousine. His grandmother eagerly waited to find out who Alex would be taking to the

prom. But to her great surprise, he told her that he would be taking her to prom.

He told her that every woman deserves to go to prom, no matter if they are 18 or 80.

"The good things in life are better with you."

-Unknown

Day 78 ☼ Date Idea   /   /

Cuddle and Movies

Why spend on cinemas when you can just set up some movies at home and snuggle nonstop with your partner? Make sure to prep some snacks you can both munch into!

His take on the date idea...   **Her take on the date idea...**

Day 79 ☼ On the Rocks   /   /

How do you fix misunderstandings within your relationship?

Others prefer to take some time away from each other, while others do not want to end the day without fixing things out. What about you?

His Answer...   **Her Answer...**

"Love is space and time measured by the heart."

-Marcel Proust

Day 80 ☼ One of a Kind   /   /

What makes your relationship unique?

Every relationship is special, but what do you think makes your relationship unique? Is it the way you fix problems, or the way you communicate with each other?

His Answer...   **Her Answer...**

Day 81 ☼ Being Free   /   /

How do you define freedom?

Just because you are in a relationship doesn't mean you'll have full control of your partner's life. Giving them the freedom to do things their way is an essential part of building your life together. What is your definition of freedom?

His Answer...   **Her Answer...**

"To love and be loved is to feel the sun from both sides."

-David Viscott

Day 82 ☼ Pet Lover   /   /

What is your favorite pet?

Aside from its cuteness, taking care of a pet together can be a way to test each other's patience. Are both of you animal lovers?

His Answer...   **Her Answer...**

Day 83 ☼ Arguments   /   /

What was your biggest fight?

Arguments and misunderstandings are part of any relationship; you just have to be respectful of your partner's decision and be considerate enough not to say hurtful things when both of your emotions are still high. What was the biggest fight you ever had?

His Answer...   **Her Answer...**

"Anyone can be passionate, but it takes real loves to be silly."

-Rose Franken

Day 84 ☼ Photo Prompt

/ /

Go pick your favorite family picture. Tell your partner why the family should always come first. Then, share with him/her the kind of family that you want to have in the future.

"Once upon a time there was a boy who loved a girl,
and her laughter was a question he wanted to spend his whole life answering."

-Nicole Krauss

Accident With A Happy Ending

When Frank's wife had a car accident, she was so injured that she fell into a coma. Years passed but Frank did not stop visiting his wife at the hospital. Even though almost everyone – including the doctors – had given up hope, he remained faithful that she would one day recover. Every time he visited her, he began talking to her, recounting all those beautiful moments they spend with each other.

One day, when he showed her the video of their wedding day, she slowly began to move her hand. She whispered his name and began gaining consciousness. Several weeks after she had woken up, she had fully recovered and was finally allowed to leave the hospital for good.

When the couple left, she told Frank that she heard his voice while she was in a coma and that it was his voice that was the greatest aid in helping her to return to consciousness.

"Maybe you don't need the whole world to love you, you know, maybe you just need one *person."*

-Kermit the Frog

Day 85 ☼ Date Idea   /   /

Dance the Night Away

You don't have to be a good dancer; you just have to intimately sway your body and be as close as you can with your partner's. You may even be surprised how turned on you might get.

His take on the date idea...   **Her take on the date idea...**

Day 86 ☼ Jealousy   /   /

What is your take on jealousy?

Jealousy is healthy, granting that you sit and discuss it, rather than succumb to your negative emotions. Are you the jealous type of partner? How do you deal with such feeling?

His Answer...   **Her Answer...**

"A boat needs the river to keep floating and I need you for my heart to keep beating."

-Marjorie Jacobs

Day 87 ☼ Lesson Learned   1 / 4 / 2021

Any relationship lesson you learned the hard way?

Sometimes, we get knocked down several times before realizing what life is trying

to teach us. Have you acquired any life lesson the hard way, which involves your

current relationship?

His Answer...

One relationship lesson I learned was that my opinion isn't the only one that matters. This is my first serious relationship, so it took some time to get used to the fact that I can't be right/come first all the time.

Her Answer...

My relationship lesson that I learned the hard way is that a lot of times the best thing you can do for yourself + your partner is let go — let go of needing to be right, old habits, and sometimes each other.

Day 88 ☼ Judgments   /   /

Do you ever compare yourself with others?

Comparisons are not always negative; if done carefully, it could actually help you

work on your shortcomings. But what is your take on this? Do you sometimes

compare yourself and feel insecure, or discover things you want to change?

His Answer...   **Her Answer...**

"You had to know a person well to make them laugh like that."

-Cassandra Clare

Day 89 ☼ The Thrills   /   /

What makes a relationship exciting?

They say the sense of excitement fades away as soon as you get too comfortable with each other. But it doesn't apply to everyone. Keeping a relationship is a continuous process; you have to work on it on a daily basis to keep the spark alive. What do you do in order to put a little more excitement in your relationship?

His Answer...   **Her Answer...**

Day 90 ☼ Looking Back   /   /

Let's say you're now on your 70's. What are the 3 things you would probably enjoy reminiscing?

It could be the day you celebrated your first anniversary or the day you sneaked out of the house just to go on late night stroll. What do you think are the memories that would make you smile just by remembering how fun it was?

His Answer...   **Her Answer...**

"You are, and always have been, my dream."

-Nicholas Sparks

Day 91 ☼ Photo Prompt

If you can recreate a photo of you together taken years ago, what photo would that be and why?

"The real lover is the man who can thrill you by kissing your forehead or smiling into your eyes or just staring into space."

-Marilyn Monroe

Lovely Poems

The poem was beautiful. She imagined what it would be like to have someone love her enough to write a poem like that about her. What she didn't realize until much later is that someone already had and she had just read it.

"Love at first sight is easy to understand; it's when two people have been looking at each other for a lifetime that it becomes a miracle."

-Sam Levenson

Day 92 ☼ Date Idea   /   /

Walk/Jog Date

Isn't it nice to just walk around without a particular destination and watch the sun together as it rises? Yes, old school, right?

His take on the date idea...   **Her take on the date idea...**

Day 93 ☼ Letting Go   /   /

Is there something you've been holding inside you that you want to let go?
Sometimes, we prefer to keep our emotions to ourselves just to avoid misunderstandings and confrontation. But take this chance to finally get it off your chest – this could be a good time to discuss it with your partner and hopefully find a way to settle things out.

His Answer...   **Her Answer...**

"Love is when he gives you a piece of your soul, that you never knew was missing."
-Torquato Tasso

Day 94 ☼ Happiness / /

What are the things you're most grateful for?

We are indeed thankful for the gift of love; thankful for the presence of our family and friends. But aside from these, what are the other things that you are grateful about?

His Answer...

Her Answer...

Day 95 ☼ Legacy 1 / 1 / 21

How do you want people to remember you?

We all want to live a happy life, but when the end comes, how do you want to be remembered, especially by your loved ones?

His Answer...

I want to be remembered as a hard worker, a creative soul, and someone with an open heart. I want my loved ones to know that I would do anything for them, no matter how ridiculous it may be. I also want to be remembered as a reliable person who always showed up when needed.

Her Answer...

I WANT TO BE REMEMBERED AS TRYING TO MAKE THE WORLD A BETTER PLACE & INSPIRE THE PEOPLE I LEAVE BEHIND TO FIGHT OPPRESSION IN ALL ITS FORMS.

I WOULD ALSO LIKE PEOPLE TO DESCRIBE ME AS FUNNY, SMART & GOOD TASTE IN MUSIC AND UNIQUE!

"The most precious possession that ever comes to a man in this world is a woman's heart."

-Josiah Holland

Day 96 ☼ The Reason   /   /

Have you discovered your purpose in life?

We all need a particular purpose to keep going, but if you haven't found yours, it's totally fine. So long as you constantly strive to find happiness in everything you do.

His Answer...   **Her Answer...**

Day 97 ☼ Excellence   /   /

What is your take on "perfection"?

Some people work so hard to be the perfect version of themselves, but do you think perfection is really necessary to keep a relationship smooth-sailing?

His Answer...   **Her Answer...**

"If I had a flower for every time I thought of you…I could walk through my garden forever."

-Alfred Tennyson

Day 98 ☼ Photo Prompt

Now let us be more creative with our photoactivity. Pick a solo photo of your partner and share your first impression of him/her. How did this impression change over time?

"No, this trick won't work.. How on earth are you ever going to explain in terms of chemistry and physics so important a biological phenomenon as first love?"

-Alber Einstein

Silent Love

He never told her he loved her. He made her coffee in the morning.

He brought her tissues when she sniffled. He bought her flowers when she was sad.

He made her favorite dinner every Tuesday, and tucked her in when she fell asleep reading.

But he never told her he loved her.

"You've gotta dance like there's nobody watching, love like you'll never be hurt,

sing like there's nobody listening, and live like it's heaven on earth."

-Willliam W. Purkey

Day 99 ☼ Date Idea   /   /

Picnic Date

When was the last time you've been on a picnic? Make sure to be updated with the weather forecast in order to avoid packing things early just because it started raining.

His take on the date idea...   **Her take on the date idea...**

Day 100 ☼ Life Morals   /   /

Top 5 life values to live by.

Faithfulness, appreciation, and respect – these are just a few great values we should apply in our lives. What 5 life values should we put into practice in order to live a joyous life?

His Answer...   **Her Answer...**

"There are never enough I Love You's."

-Lenny Bruce

Day 101 ☼ Character   /   /

Describe yourself in 3 words.

Do not be conscious. What do you think are the 3 words that would best describe your personality?

His Answer...   **Her Answer...**

Day 102 ☼ Perfect You   /   /

Describe your partner in 3 words.

Your partner may be interested to hear how you describe him/her to other people. What 3 words would best describe his/her personality?

His Answer...   **Her Answer...**

"It doesn't matter who you are or what you look like, so long as somebody loves you."

-Ronald Dahl

Day 103 ☼ Outlook   /   /

How do you see yourself 10 years from now?

Are you looking forward to having a family by this time? Or would you like to take your time and focus on your career first? Either way, how different do you think things will be a decade from now?

His Answer...   **Her Answer...**

Day 104 ☼ Inspiration   /   /

What makes you leap out of bed every morning?

Set a goal that would motivate you to always start your day right. What are the things that make you roll up your sleeves on a daily basis?

His Answer...   **Her Answer...**

"The heart has reasons that reason cannot know."

-Pascal

Day 105 ☼ Photo Prompt / /

Can you find some stolen shots on your album/camera roll? Choose your favorite one and why do you think this photo was so candid?

"If I could reach up and hold a star for every time you've made me smile,
the entire evening sky would be in the palm of my hand."

-Anonymous

Grateful Tears

"Mom, why does this song make you cry?"

"It reminds me of someone."

"Someone who made you sad?"

"No. Someone who made me very, very happy."

"When someone loves you, the way they say your name is different.

You know that your name is safe in their mouth."

-Jess C. Scott

Day 106 ☼ Date Idea   /   /

Art Class Date

If you aren't a good painter, don't worry. You can pretend what you created was an abstract and try to interpret the meaning on your own. Kidding aside, it's always fun to express ourselves through colorful arts.

His take on the date idea...   **Her take on the date idea...**

Day 107 ☼ Accomplishments   /   /

If you only have 5 days to live, what would you like to get done?

List down the things that you want to accomplish if you have a limited time to live; would you rather spend your last moments with your family? Or would you finally do that once-in-a-lifetime adventure you've always dreaded?

His Answer...   **er Answer...**

"Love is but the discovery of ourselves in others, and the delight in the recognition."

-Alexander Smith

Day 108 ☼ Setting Priorities / /

What are your priorities and how do you set them straight?

Setting your priorities straight is one important key to reaching your goals, particularly if your daily routine or workload tends to be really hefty. What are your priorities at the moment?

His Answer...   **Her Answer...**

Day 109 ☼ Feeling Lucky / /

Was there a time when you felt really lucky?

This is just for fun: Have you ever had a stroke of luck and won something by chance? Some people even believe in lucky charms. Tell us about that time when you felt so lucky.

His Answer...   **Her Answer...**

"To love deeply in one direction makes us more loving in all others."

-Anne Sophie Swetchine

Day 110 ☼ Acceptance   /   /

Has the society ever put pressure on you?

The need to conform to what the society generally believes to be right or acceptable could be really stressful. Have you ever felt that kind of pressure? How do you/would you handle this?

His Answer...   **Her Answer...**

Day 111 ☼ Quotable Quote   /   /

What is your favorite quote or book excerpt?

We sometimes find lines from books and movies that are worth pondering on. What is your favorite and how were you able to relate to it?

His Answer...   **Her Answer...**

"One is loved because one is loved. No reason is needed for loving."

-Paulo Coelho

Day 112 ☼ Photo Prompt

Choose a photo that shows something you're passionate about. We'd love to hear about it.

"When I am with you, we stay up all night. When you're not here, I can't go to sleep. Praise God for those two insomnias! And the difference between them."

-Rumi

Everlasting

Her hand was not as pretty as it had been. It was wrinkled and blotchy.

Still, when he held it in his own wrinkled hand it felt the same as always.

"If there ever comes a day when we can't be together, keep me in your heart,

I'll stay there forever."

-A.A. Milne

Day 113 ☼ Date Idea   /   /

Sports Date

Try to come up with a sport that you both like and figure out who needs to practice some more.

His take on the date idea...   **Her take on the date idea...**

Day 114 ☼ Self-Awareness   /   /

What is mankind's greatest enemy?

How aware are you of your surroundings? There are bigger things that are happening outside your domain. What do you think is our biggest adversary?

His Answer...   **Her Answer...**

"To love abundantly is to live abundantly, and to love forever is to live forever."

-Henry Drummond

Day 115 ☼ Transformation   /   /

Any bad habit you want to break?

Bad habits come in different forms: It could be in a form of vices like smoking and too much drinking or behavioral issues like procrastination. Either way, they could delay your personal progress and affect your life for the long haul. What bad habit/s do you want to break and how do you plan to do it?

His Answer...   **Her Answer...**

Day 116 ☼ Modern Advancement   /   /

How does technology affect personal relationships?

Technology definitely makes our lives easier. But was there a time when you felt like it is becoming more of a problem that affects relationships? If so, in what way?

His Answer...   **Her Answer...**

"I love you not only for what you are, but for what I am when I am with you."

-Elizabeth Barrett Browning

Day 117 ☼ Changes   /   /

Have you [recently] lost interest in something you used to enjoy?

As we grow older and become more mature, we tend to lose interests in things we used to have fun doing – like playing video games, for example. Have this ever happened to you, or do you feel like you're actually starting to feel this way?

His Answer...   **Her Answer...**

Day 118 ☼ The Best Day   /   /

What is your most favorite time of the year?

Is it your anniversary, or do you value Christmas, most of all? How do you celebrate your favorite time of the year, and why do you consider it special?

His Answer...   **Her Answer...**

"I love you. I am at rest with you. I have come home."

-Dorothy L. Sayers

Day 119 ☼ Photo Prompt

Choose 3 to 5 photos that show things or people who are close to your heart. We'd be really happy to hear why they are so special.

"For it was not into my ear you whispered, but into my heart.

It was not my lips you kissed, but my soul."

-Judy Garland

Embracing Uncertainty

I had dreams. I had my life all planned out, but I did not plan for this.

I did not plan for you. I'm abandoning everything I thought I wanted,

but your love has taught me I wasn't dreaming big enough.

"I love you. I am who I am because of you. You are every reason, every hope, and every dream I've ever

had, and no matter what happens to us in the future, everyday we are together

is the greatest day of my life. I will always be yours."

-Nicholas Sparks

Day 120 ☼ Date Idea   /   /

Breakfast Date

When you had a nice breakfast, you're actually off to a good start. Wake up early and visit the nearest coffee shop. Exchange updates on each other's life.

His take on the date idea...   **Her take on the date idea...**

Day 121 ☼ Fight   /   /

When was the last time you argued with someone (not necessarily your partner)?

Arguments are inevitable, but there is nothing a good communication can't resolve. Do you remember the reason behind this misunderstanding? How did you resolve it? What lessons have you learned after patching things up?

His Answer...   **Her Answer...**

"You are like nobody since I love you."

-Pablo Neruda

Day 122 ☼ Goal Unmet / /

Is there anything you wish you had accomplished earlier in life?

Not everyone gets to accomplish their goals on time. Many of us get stuck and go through an enormous amount of trials before being successful. What about you?

His Answer...   **Her Answer...**

Day 123 ☼ Just for Love / /

What's the craziest, or perhaps the most illogical thing you did for love?

Admit it or not, most of us go through that phase where we are willing to go beyond our limitations just to prove how much we love someone. What's your story?

His Answer...   **Her Answer...**

"I love you and it's getting worse."

-Joseph E. Morris

Day 124 ☼ Young at Heart   /   /

What is the most childish yet fun thing you did with your partner?

It could be as simple as playing/dancing in the rain, or running in the park like little kids. Reminisce that one childish moment with your partner and how much you enjoyed it.

His Answer...   **Her Answer...**

Day 125 ☼ Unwind   /   /

What is your favorite go-to place to relieve stress?

To relax with your loved one is probably what we need after a long, tiring week. Where is your favorite place to de-stress?

His Answer...   **Her Answer...**

"I love you for all that you are, all that you have been and all you are yet to be."

-Unknown

Day 126 ☼ Photo Prompt   /   /

Can you pick a photo from your album that shows a place you consider special? It could be your old family house in the countryside or that vacant lot you used to play at with your childhood friends.

"I love you without knowing how, or when, or from where. I love you simply, without problems or pride: I love you in this way because I do not know any other way of loving but this, in which there is no I or you, so intimate that your hand upon my chest is my hand, so intimate that when I fall asleep your eyes close."

-Pablo Neruda

Keeping What Was Good

After he was gone she no longer thought about the imperfections of their imperfect life together. She remembered being happy together, and that was enough.

"I love you also means I love you more than anyone loves you, or has loved you, or will love you, and also, I love you in a way that no one loves you, or has loved you, or will love you, and also, I love you in a way that I love no one else, and never have loved anyone else, and never will love anyone else."

-Jonathan Safran Foer

Day 127 ☼ Date Idea   /   /

Go on a Road Trip

Windows down with sounds at full blast – sometimes, we just need to temporarily escape from our busy lives in order to get our priorities straight once again.

His take on the date idea...   **Her take on the date idea...**

Day 128 ☼ What Ifs   /   /

If you were given the chance to know the answer to just one specific question, what would that question be?

Every one of us surely has that one question in mind that we've been dying to know the answer about. Ponder on this carefully. What exactly would you like to find out?

His Answer...   **Her Answer...**

For you see, each day I love you more. Today more than yesterday and less than tomorrow."

-Rosemonde Gerard

Day 129 ☼ Lapses   /   /

Are you afraid to make mistakes?

And what kind of mistake, to be exact, do you fear to commit? What do you do in order to avoid such thing?

His Answer...   **Her Answer...**

Day 130 ☼ Devotions   /   /

Are you afraid of commitments?

Why are you or aren't you afraid of it? What do you think are the things you need to consider before entering any commitment?

His Answer...   **Her Answer...**

"I love you much (most beautiful darling) more than anyone on the earth

and I like you better than everything in the sky."

-E.E. Cummings

Day 131 ☼ Getting Cozy   /   /

What is your guilty pleasure?

We all have that activity we feel ashamed of telling people about. Yet sooner or later, you'll be comfortable enough to share it with your partner, no matter how weird or funny it is. What is yours?

His Answer...   **Her Answer...**

Day 132 ☼ Being Bossy   /   /

When do you usually feel dominant?

Not necessarily within your relationship – it could be at work or in a sport you're really good at. When do you feel powerful, and how does it boost your self-esteem?

His Answer...   **Her Answer...**

"I love you, and I will love you until I die, and if there's a life after that, I'll love you then.*"*

-Cassandra Clare

Day 133 ☼ Photo Prompt

Have you kept any photo that somehow describes your past? If not, try to imagine a particular scenario in your head and help us picture it out.

"I love you in a weak at my knees, butterflies in my stomach,
giddy little kid in a candy store kind of way."

-Unknown

Passion

"I never thought you liked me," she gasped between kisses.

"No," he said,

" I like you very much."

So they kept on kissing.

"I never loved you any more than I do, right this second.
And I'll never love you any less than I do, right this second."

-Kami Garcia & Margaret Stohl

Day 134 ☼ Date Idea   /   /

Karaoke Date

Without judging each other's singing skills, belt out on difficult songs and laugh at each other!

His take on the date idea...   **Her take on the date idea...**

Day 135 ☼ Hideaway   /   /

What is one thing that you and your partner always find worth your time and effort?

Is it quick date night amidst the busy week, or maybe a weekend getaway to temporarily shut yourselves off from work-related stress?.

His Answer...   **Her Answer...**

"I am catastrophically in love with you."

-Cassandra Clare

Day 136 ☼ Staycation   /   /

How do you make your weekend relaxing without having to leave the house and spend money?

Do you enjoy binge-watching a really good series while snuggling next to your loved one? Ah, sounds perfect. Do you have other ideas on how to make your weekend worthwhile?

His Answer...   **Her Answer...**

Day 137 ☼ Motivation   /   /

List down the people that come into your mind when you think of success.
It must be the people who helped you pick yourself up during a difficult time or those who believed in you when circumstances tell them otherwise.

His Answer...   **Her Answer...**

"I love you more than there are stars in the sky and fish in the sea."
-Nicholas Sparks

Day 138 ☼ Just for Keeps   /   /

List down the things you currently have that you're afraid of losing.

It could be your job or a really strong friendship. Ponder on the things you have at the moment that you think you can't afford to lose.

His Answer...   **Her Answer...**

Day 139 ☼ Big Decision   /   /

Are you willing to give up a really stable job in exchange for happiness?

People are inclined to stick to a job they do not necessarily love just because it is practical to do so. Are you willing to give it up in order to acquire happiness and satisfaction, despite not being sure what the future holds?

His Answer...   **Her Answer...**

"I love you more than I have ever found a way to say to you."

-Ben Folds

Day 140 ☼ Photo Prompt

Pick a photo of you taken about 3 years ago (or more). Tell us how your old version of the picture differs from what you are right now.

"When I tell you I love you, I don't say it out of habit.
I say it to remind you that you are the best thing that has ever happened to me."
-Unknown

A Dream Come True

The two men held the paper tightly as if it could disappear at any moment.

They barely believed that after so many years together they were finally married.

Really married.

They kissed again as the boy clapped joyfully.

"I've never had a moment's doubt. I love you. I believe in you completely.

You are my dearest one, my reason for life."

-Ian McEwan

Day 141 ☼ Date Idea   /   /

Ice Cream Date

You will probably enjoy that afternoon walk in the park with a big cone of ice cream in hand!

His take on the date idea...   **Her take on the date idea...**

Day 142 ☼ The Spark   /   /

Do you believe in love at first sight?

Some people vouch that it is totally possible to feel a connection during the first meeting, while others believe you have to take enough time to know the person first. What can you say about this? How did this work for you, based on your personal experience?

His Answer...   **Her Answer...**

"Why do I love you? Because you are and always have been my dream."

-Unknown

Day 143 ☼ The Mark   /   /

Does first impression really last?

If for some reason, someone has a really bad first impression on you, do you think you can still find a way to change it? Or will this be your permanent image to them?

His Answer...   **Her Answer...**

Day 144 ☼ Unforgettable Moment   /   /

What is the most terrifying experience you had in your life?

Try to recall the incident; how did you react to it? Did it affect you in any way [emotionally, mentally or physically]? Have you acquired any lesson from it?

His Answer...   **Her Answer...**

"I love you as certain dark things are to be loved, in secret, between the shadow and the soul."

-Pablo Neruda

Day 145 ☼ Survival   /   /

Through all the life's hardships, what made you persevere and survive?

Do you sometimes have that moment where you look back at all the things you've gone through and ask, "how did I survive all that?" How did you manage to keep going?

His Answer...   **Her Answer...**

Day 146 ☼ Getting Sick   /   /

When was the last time you got sick that you had to skip going to work?

When you are healthy, you are capable of achieving a lot of things, especially at work. Health is definitely one's wealth, so investing in your well-being is an essential part of becoming successful. How do you take care of yourself as well?

His Answer...   **Her Answer...**

"So, I love you because the entire universe conspired to help me find you."

-Paulo Coelho

Day 147 ☼ Photo Prompt   /   /

Proudly share a photo that shows a physically different version of yourself – like the time you gained some weight, the time you shaved or cut your hair really short or when you wore something that is not really your style.

"I Love You. That's my secret. No hearts, no pretty drawings.
No poems or cryptic messages… I Love You."
-Nikhil Saluja

Let Love Go

He let her go because it was what she wanted.

She didn't realize until too late that was exactly why she should have stayed.

"Love is too weak a word for what I feel. I luuurve you, you know, I loave you, I luff you, two F's, yes I have to invent, of course I do, don't you think I do?"

-Woody Allen

Day 148 ☼ Date Idea   /   /

Go on a Hike

Aside from being close to nature, hiking will give you a strong sense of accomplishment once you experience reaching the summit – now imagine being on the very top with your loved one!

His take on the date idea...   **Her take on the date idea...**

Day 149 ☼ Being Upset   /   /

What is the most embarrassing situation you've been in?

Everyone has their fair share of embarrassing moments. What' is yours, and how did you handle it? Does it still feel awkward whenever you think about it?

His Answer...   **Her Answer...**

"I love you no matter what you do, but do you have to do so much of it?"

-Jean Illsley Clarke

Day 150 ☼ Fit Together / /

What kind of sports do you enjoy doing/playing together?

Staying fit is one goal a couple can enjoy. Have you tried playing any sports, or at least willing to try one?

His Answer... **Her Answer...**

Day 151 ☼ Delight / /

What particular thing do you do just to please your partner?

You can cook and prep a romantic dinner at home; you may also prep a romantic movie with a bottle of wine. What do you do to please him/her once in awhile?

His Answer... **Her Answer...**

"I love you, in my mind where my thoughts reside, in my heart where my emotions live, and in my soul where my dreams are born. I love you."

-Dee Henderson

Day 152 ☼ Trust Issues   /   /

What do you do when your partner commits a mistake that basically affects your trust?

Do wait until your anger subsides? Or do you confront him/her right then and there? How do you deal with a damaged trust?

His Answer...　　　　　　　　　　　**Her Answer...**

Day 153 ☼ Second Chances   /   /

When do you think someone deserves a second chance?

They say we all deserve a second chance, but what are the factors you need to consider before deciding whether or not you should give someone that chance.

His Answer...　　　　　　　　　　　**Her Answer...**

"Do I love you because you're beautiful, or are you beautiful because I love you?"

-Richard Rodgers

Day 154 ☼ Photo Prompt   /   /

What is the most random photo (solo or together) you can find on your album or camera roll?

"I have never had anyone love me the way you love me.
I have never loved anyone the way I love you.
Thank you God for showing us the way to each other."

-Nishan Panwar

Bonds Grow Through Time

They say that absence makes the heart grow fonder, but for them it was proximity.

At first they barely liked each other, but after years of working side-by-side

their emerging fondness for one another became too strong to ignore.

"Immature love says: 'I love you because I need you.'

Mature love says 'I need you because I love you.'"

-Erich Fromm

Day 155 ☼ Date Idea   /   /

Set up Your Own Photography Session

What's even lovelier about this date idea is that you've got your partner to be your photography subject. Trust each other's skills and give your best shot!

His take on the date idea...   **Her take on the date idea...**

Day 156 ☼ Expression of Love   /   /

What is your take on public display of affection?

Depending on the country you're from or the culture you grew up with – showing your love and affection in a place where people can easily see it may not be normal for others. Some people think it's embarrassing, while some think there's nothing wrong with trying to express how they feel, even if it's in public.

His Answer...   **Her Answer...**

"I wonder if it's possible to have a love affair that lasts forever."

-Andy Warhol

Day 157 ☼ Familiarity   /   /

How much does your partner know about your life?

Does your partner know about your childhood? About your life as a student, up until you two met each other? Or are there things that may take a little more time before you feel comfortable sharing?

His Answer...   **Her Answer...**

Day 158 ☼ Confidant   /   /

Who do you seek advice from when you have a misunderstanding with your partner?

Many of us usually confide our worries to our closest/best friends, while some prefer sharing with their parents. Who do you usually go to when you needed a friendly relationship advice?

His Answer...   **Her Answer...**

"You will forever be my always."

-Unknown

Day 159 ☼ Going Out   /   /

Would you consider camping together?

They say taking some time off from the internet and all your gadgets may help you regain a healthy body clock and reinvigorate your body and mind. How does outdoor camping sound to you?

His Answer...   **Her Answer...**

Day 160 ☼ Treasured Moments   /   /

What is the most fun memory you had of high school or college?

We all go through that phase of confusion during our teenage years, but what's important is that we were at our bravest to try new things despite not knowing what's in store for us. When you think of high school or college, what is the fondest or funniest thing that comes to your mind?

His Answer...   **Her Answer...**

"They say nothing lasts forever, we'll have to prove them wrong."

-Unknown

Day 161 ☼ Photo Prompt   /   /

Aside from the personal photos kept in your album, have you tried amateur photography? What kind of photoshoot subject would you like to work on?

"When you realize you want to spend the rest of your life with a person, you want the rest of your life to start as soon as possible."

-Billy Crystal

Love is Felt, Not Seen

He never thought she was beautiful. He thought she was smart. He thought she was funny.

He thought she was kinder than he deserved, but he never thought she was beautiful.

He knew she was beautiful. Even as a blind man he could see that.

"There is no pretending. I love you, and I will love you until I die,

and if there is life after that, I'll love you then."

-Cassandra Clare

Day 162 ☼ Date Idea   /   /

Boat Ride

Slowly move that paddle while enjoying each other's company – this could be the perfect time to enjoy sharing stories, particularly when you've both been busy in the past few weeks.

His take on the date idea...   **Her take on the date idea...**

Day 163 ☼ Romance   /   /

What was the most romantic date you had?

This depends on your concept of "romantic" – but when was the time you went out on a date that you think was really romantic?

His Answer...   **Her Answer...**

"He is not a lover who does not love forever."

-Euripedes

Day 164 ☼ Consistency   /   /

Do you think you are able to express your love on a daily basis?

You can express your love in many different ways, but do you think you are expressive enough to let your partner know how much you appreciate him/her everyday?

His Answer...   **Her Answer...**

Day 165 ☼ Three Words   /   /

When was the last time you said: "I love you"?

Some people may not be vocal enough to express their love through words. When was the last time you told your partner you love him/her and why do you think we need to say it once in awhile?

His Answer...   **Her Answer...**

"Love is forever, and if it doesn't last forever it isn't love."

-Dottie Kinnealy

Day 166 ☼ Realizations   /   /

How and when did you realize that you have fallen in love with your partner?

Did you feel, right away, that there was a certain connection between you two? Or did it take you a few months before officially becoming a couple?

His Answer...   **Her Answer...**

Day 167 ☼ Changes   /   /

List down 5 ways your life has changed since your partner came.

A good partner is someone who brings out the best in you. How has your life changed since you found the love of your life? Were the changes all worth it?

His Answer...   **Her Answer...**

"I could lay next to you forever... or until we decide to go eat."

-Unknown

Day 168 ☼ Photo Prompt

Okay, this should be fun! Pick a random photo and make up your own (silly) story that would best suit your partner's pose or facial expression in the picture.

"As the train was passing by and you left, I was looking for that last glance of you. I was thinking of all the reasons why I feel in love with you and did not even realize how an hour passed by. That is how much I love you."

-Gilead Zoo

True Love Never Dies

She continued to mourn him, but she was not the only one who mourned.

So did the men who came later and found they could never compete with the dead man

who still held her heart.

"I loved you like a man loves a woman he never touches, only writes to,

keeps little photographs of."

-Charles Bukowski

Day 169 ☼ Date Idea   /   /

Attend a Seminar Together

Seminars can be boring – but not when you attend it together. Did you learn how to create a sales pitch? Did you acquire a new skill? There's just one way to find out!

His take on the date idea...   **Her take on the date idea...**

Day 170 ☼ The First Date   /   /

How did your first date go?

Was it a failure, or did it go exactly as planned? First dates are always one of the most fun memories to reminisce.

His Answer...   **Her Answer...**

"I love you more than I think I should."

-Becca Fitzpatrick

Day 171 ☼ Giving Back / /

Have you done any voluntary work together, or at least planning to join one?

Helping others is more fun when you get to do it with your loved one. What charity work or institution would you like to volunteer too?

His Answer...   Her Answer...

Day 172 ☼ Approval / /

When your friends do not like your partner, does it really matter?

Sometimes, our friends and partner just do not have many similarities that they end up not liking each other very well. It is something that we can easily work on, but does it really bother you at all?

His Answer...   Her Answer...

"To say 'I love you' one must first be able to say the 'I.'"

-Ayn Rand

Day 173 ☼ Indifferences   /   /

How similar or different are your religious beliefs?

Does it affect your relationship in general, or do you prefer not to discuss it? Do you think it is going to be easy being in a relationship with someone who holds a strong, opposite belief than yours?

His Answer...   **Her Answer...**

Day 174 ☼ Sacrifices   /   /

In what way do you think you have proven your love to your partner?

Sometimes, we need to sacrifice things or tolerate unwanted circumstances just to be with the person we love. What have you done to prove that you are serious about your relationship?

His Answer...   **Her Answer...**

"Love is a brief moment for which you hold forever."

-Unknown

Day 175 ☼ Photo Prompt   /   /

Share a certain family tradition in your household while holding up a picture of you with your closest relatives. This can be a good way to let your partner know more about the family who raised you.

"The saddest thing about love… is that not only the love cannot last forever, but even the heartbreak is soon forgotten."

-William Faulkner

Let It All Out

He looked better than she remembered,

and she had remembered him often.

She always wondered what would have happened

if she had told him how she felt about him.

Well, tonight she intended to find out.

(She would be pleased with the result.)

"I love you, and because I love you, I would sooner have you hate me

for telling you the truth than adore me for telling you lies."

-Pietro Aretino

Day 176 ☼ Date Idea   /   /

Arcade Date

Compete for the highest score. Whoever loses will buy dinner! – And that's probably the girl.

His take on the date idea...   **Her take on the date idea...**

Day 177 ☼ Meet the Parents   /   /

When is the perfect time to bring our partner home and meet the rest of your family?

This may be a sensitive thing to discuss, but remember that we also aim to stretch your understanding and maturity through this question.

His Answer...   **Her Answer...**

"Hello, I love you. Won't you tell me your name? Hello, I love you. Let me jump in your game."

-The Doors

Day 178 ☼ Practices   /   /

What family tradition would you like to share with your partner?

Personal traditions make every family unique. What tradition would you introduce to your partner and who did you choose it?

His Answer...   **Her Answer...**

Day 179 ☼ The First Gift   /   /

Tell us the story behind your first gift.

Choosing the first present during the early stage of your relationship can be quite stressful, mainly because you're still trying to figure out what he/she likes and not. Share with us how you come up with that first present and how did your partner react to it.

His Answer...   **Her Answer...**

"An eternity is forever, and forever with you would be a dream come true."

-Daniel

Day 180 ☼ Investment   /   /

What was the first possession you had as a couple?

What was the first thing you bought by putting your money or savings together?

How did it feel to have someone to share expenses or responsibilities with?

His Answer...   **Her Answer...**

Day 181 ☼ The Photo   /   /

Share your favorite photo together.

What was your favorite shot and when or where was it taken? Tell us the story

behind it; there must be a reason why you consider it as your favorite.

His Answer...   **Her Answer...**

"Two lives, two hearts joined together in friendship united forever in love."

-Dottie Kinealy

Day 182 ☼ Photo Prompt   /   /

Still using the same family picture you consider your favorite, introduce each member to your partner. You may include some of your distant relatives if you like.

"I love you because no two snowflakes are alike, and it is possible, if you stand tippy-toe, to walk between the raindrops."

-Nikki Giovanni

Better Than A Movie

"If this were a movie we'd probably kiss now."

"Too bad this isn't a movie, huh?"

"Yep."

He took her hand as they walked and laughed.

And although they did not have their movie kiss at that moment,

they would have many to come as they headed toward

a happy ending that no movie could match.

"Do I love you? My God, if your love were a grain of sand,

mine would be a universe of beaches."

-William Goldman

Day 183 ☼ Date Idea   /   /

Watch the Sunset

You don't have to be on the beach side to enjoy the romantic feels. Waiting for the sun to rise at your own balcony, or at the rooftop can be equally romantic.

His take on the date idea...   **Her take on the date idea...**

Day 184 ☼ Significant Other   /   /

Is it okay for your partner to have a best friend from the opposite sex?

Some people have trust issues; they do not feel comfortable over the fact that their partner spends a lot of time hanging out with a close friend from the opposite sex. What is your take on this?

His Answer...   **Her Answer...**

"I can't promise you forever, because that's not long enough."

-Jasinda Wilder

Day 185 ☼ Destiny / /

Do you believe in a soul mate?

What is your definition of a soul mate? Do you believe that there is really someone out there who is destined to be our lifetime partner?

His Answer...   **Her Answer...**

Day 186 ☼ Being Romantic / /

What was the most romantic thing you did for the sake of love?

Men are probably not very comfortable with this question, but let's admit, love can make us go crazy. You are going to cry when it hurts, no matter how big or masculine you are. What was the mushiest thing you did just to make your partner happy?

His Answer...   **Her Answer...**

"Time doesn't matter love is forever."

-Unknown

Day 187 ☼ Great Escape   /   /

What is your dream vacation as a couple?

Do you dream of traveling abroad together? Or a simple getaway where you can indulge in physical pleasure like massage or spa is much better?

His Answer...   **Her Answer...**

Day 188 ☼ Love Drunk   /   /

Have you ever got so drunk together?

Have you two had a night out where you got so drunk and careless together? It's probably messy but it's the memories that count.

His Answer...   **Her Answer...**

"...on forever's very now we stand."

-E.E. Cummings

Day 189 ☼ Photo Prompt   /   /

Do you have a photo of your workmates? Trust issues that are related to work are common in a relationship. You may take this chance to let your partner know that he/she can trust the people you work with.

"With all my heart, and all my soul, I will love you till the winds don't blow. Until the oceans turn to stone, my love is yours and yours alone. My love is forever, until forever's gone."

-Kenny Rogers

Expressing Love

As she walked away he grabbed her arm and told her to stay.

He said "You're not pretty, you're beautiful. I don`t want to be with you forever, I need to

be with you forever. And I wouldn't cry if you walked away, I would die."

"It isn't possible to love and part. You will wish that it was. You can transmute love, ignore it, muddle it,

but you can never pull it out of you. I know by experience that the poets are right:

love is eternal."

-E.M. Forster

Day 190 ☼ Date Idea / /

Visit a Dog Café

Because cafes that allow you to cuddle random dogs is now a thing!

His take on the date idea...   **Her take on the date idea...**

Day 191 ☼ Attraction / /

Describe what attracts you most to a person, physically.

Try to go into detail. What physical features do you find attractive in the opposite
sex? What exactly do you find sexy?

His Answer...   **Her Answer...**

"I will love you all my life and when I die I will still love you through eternity and beyond."

-Leann

Day 192 ☼ Small Fight   /   /

What was the pettiest misunderstanding you had?

Sometimes, we act like kids and become irritated even with the most irrelevant thing. Petty fights are part of a healthy relationship, so long as you choose to settle it and laugh at how childish both of you can get at times.

His Answer...   **Her Answer...**

Day 193 ☼ My Dear   /   /

What term of endearment do you use to call each other?

Baby, sweetie, honey – these are just some of the usual endearments that couples use. Nevertheless, other couples are creative enough to come up with their own term. What is yours, and is there a significant meaning for such term?

His Answer...   **Her Answer...**

"Fall in love.. that is fine, but just make sure you fall deep enough to stay there forever."

-Ram Mohan

Day 194 ☼ Conversations   /   /

Do you enjoy engaging in intellectual conversations, or do you prefer light topics?

Are you the type of couple who doesn't mind engaging in a heated debate about religion or politics? Or do you prefer having just light and chill conversations?

His Answer...   **Her Answer...**

Day 195 ☼ Distance   /   /

What do you miss about your partner when you are not together?

They say taking some time away from each other will make you miss him/her even more. When your partner is out of reach, what do you usually yearn for him/her?

His Answer...   **Her Answer...**

"Promise me you'll never forget me because if I thought you would, I'd never leave."

—A.A. Milne

Day 196 ☼ Photo Prompt

Show us a photo that was taken during one of your date nights. What kind of date did you have the time it was taken (movie, walk in the part, etc)? Why is it good to reminisce romantic nights like this once in a while?

"If water was a kiss, I'd send you the sea. If a hug was a leaf, I'd send you a tree.

If love was forever, I'd send you eternity."

-K. Martins

How I Met Your Mother

Boy: Can I take a photo?

Girl: Why?

Boy: I just want to show my children how their mom looked when she was younger...

"If you love something let it go free. If it doesn't come back, you never had it.

If it comes back, love it forever."

-Doug Horton

Day 197 ☼ Date Idea   /   /

Salon Date

Enjoy a hair treatment or a manicure together! Just like the spa date, this is equally relaxing!

His take on the date idea...   **Her take on the date idea...**

Day 198 ☼ Sweet Surprises   /   /

Do you prefer giving/receiving flowers or something to munch on, like chocolates?

Do you know your partner well enough to come up with the best kind of present that you know he/she would appreciate?

His Answer...   **Her Answer...**

"If only for a day the two of us could be as one, then forever I would still carry that tune."

-Unknown

Day 199 ☼ Sexiness   /   /

Share 3 things about your partner that you find sexy.

It depends on how you define sexiness. It could be merely physical, or the way a person interacts with people. What 3 things do you think to make your partner really sexually attractive?

His Answer...   **Her Answer...**

Day 200 ☼ Anniversaries   /   /

How do you celebrate anniversaries?

The anniversary is perhaps the most special occasion for every couple because it reminds them how everything started – from being just friends, or officemates, to being partners in life. How do you prefer to celebrate this special day?

His Answer...   **Her Answer...**

"Romance is the glamour which turns the dust of everyday life into a golden haze."

—Elinor Glyn

Day 201 ☼ The Peak   /   /

What is the highlight of your year?

Is there any significant event that occurred this year? Or do you feel that your relationship has gotten more mature? What is the most unforgettable thing that happened to the both of you this year?

His Answer...   **Her Answer...**

Day 202 ☼ Social Media   /   /

On privacy: Do you think that couples should be open about their online activities on different social media platforms like Facebook?

This is a common issue that brings misunderstanding to many young couples. But what is your take on this? Should we allow our partners to check what we do or who we interact with online, or this is an invasion of privacy?

His Answer...   **Her Answer...**

"One word frees us of all the weight and pain of life: That word is love."

—Sophocles

Day 203 ☼ Photo Prompt   /   /

Let us get all the more creative! If you can organize a themed photo shoot with your partner, what kind of theme would you like to work on?

"My love to you is everlasting; it will never grow old and it will never fade away.

I will forever love you."

-Unknown

No Need to Be Self-Conscious

Today, after spending nearly 24 years of my life self conscious of being a 6'2 tall woman, and being taller than most of the guys, I fell in love and married a guy in a wheelchair.

"The rose that you gave me has faded, and wilted away.
But, the love tucked in deep inside remains in my heart forever."

-Unknown

Day 204 ☼ Date Idea / /

Attend a Comedy Show

Laughter will always be the best medicine. Laughing your stress away can refresh your senses, so what are you waiting for?

His take on the date idea...   **Her take on the date idea...**

Day 205 ☼ Familiarity / /

Let's see how well you know your partner: what can make him/her jump for joy?

Is it a new puppy for your girlfriend? Or a new guitar for your musically-inclined boyfriend? What kind of material things do you think can make your partner really happy?

His Answer...   **Her Answer...**

"If the only place where I could see you was in my dreams, I would sleep forever."

-Unknown

Day 206 ☼ First Love   /   /

Tell us about your first love.

This question requires utmost understanding from both sides. After all, it is just a
question meant to encourage the both of you to open up a bit more about your
past. Tell us about the first time you fell in love.

His Answer...   **Her Answer...**

Day 207 ☼ Companionship   /   /

What is your definition of a good friendship?

Every strong relationship started from friendship. If you treat each other as best
friends, it could be a solid foundation for the kind of relationship you're trying to
build. How do you define friendship in the first place?

His Answer...   **Her Answer...**

"I fell in love the way you fall asleep: slowly, and then all once..."

-John Green

Day 208 ☼ Objective Cues   /   /

How well do you know your partner's body language?

Can you tell when he/she is being jealous? Do you know when something is bothering your partner just by observing his/her gestures?

His Answer...   **Her Answer...**

Day 209 ☼ First Encounter   /   /

Do you remember the time you first met?

Was your first meeting pleasant, or one of you didn't instantly like the other? First meetings are always fun to reminisce because it reminds us just how far we've gotten since that day.

His Answer...   **Her Answer...**

"We loved with a love that was more than love."

—Edgar Allan Poe

Day 210 ☼ Photo Prompt

Among the photos that were kept in your album or camera roll, which one do you think should be put in a frame? Why would you like to display it?

"Your task is not to seek for love, but merely to seek and find all the barriers within yourself that you have built against it."

-Rumi

Bliss

Today, after dreaming about it for the last ten years, she sat down on my lap in my wheelchair with me and kissed me on the lips.

And then she paused for a second, smiled and went in for another.

*"One day you will kiss a man you can't breathe without
and find that breath is of little consequence."*
—Karen Marie Moning

Day 211 ☼ Date Idea   /   /

Visit a Museum

It may sound boring for younger people, but you gotta see a wonderful work of art at least once in your life!

His take on the date idea...   **Her take on the date idea...**

Day 212 ☼ Sense of Humor   /   /

Do you believe in the modern saying that funny is the new sexy?

Our definition of sexiness has changed over time. Many people find humor as a sexy trait; nothing beats a man/woman who can make his/her partner laugh. What is your take on this?

His Answer...   **Her Answer...**

"You are the one girl that made me risk everything for a future worth having."

—Simone Elkeles

Day 213 ☼ Lost Trust

1 / 5 / 2021

What can you do to regain your partner's trust?

Every time we commit mistakes, we also take away a portion of our partner's trust. If you do not take immediate action, this could damage the relationship in the future. What can you do in order to regain his/her lost trust?

His Answer...

- Reassurance
- Buy me coffee.
- Put in effort to change / not break trust again.
- Let time heal the wound

Her Answer...

Make me rice ☺
+ give me back scratches
+ wait
Be better/change/grow
+ have patience for the trust to come back

Day 214 ☼ Comparisons

/ /

Is life better with him or without him?

Have you ever thought of what your current life would be if you are not with your partner? Or say if you haven't met each other?

His Answer...

Her Answer...

"It was love at first sight, at last sight, at ever and ever sight."

—Vladimir Nabokov

Day 215 ☼ Working Space   /   /

Do you get inspired with your special someone working in the same place?

Do you think it's a good idea for you or other couples, in general, to be in the same workplace, or do you think they are going to be more efficient if they work separately?

His Answer...   **Her Answer...**

Day 216 ☼ Gratefulness   /   /

List down 3 random things your partner does that make you thankful and happy.

Is it when she gives you a massage after a long day at work? Or when he picks you up to make sure you get home safe? Read them aloud and take the chance to say thank you.

His Answer...   **Her Answer...**

"If I had a flower for every time I thought of you ... I could walk through my garden forever."

—Alfred Tennyson

Day 217 ☼ Photo Prompt   /   /

Do you have any photo that brings back a sad memory of the past? Go through your album and pick it up to share with us.

"If you love someone, do not put their name in a heart because hearts can be broken, instead put their name in a circle, because circles go on forever."

-Unknown

"Yes"

Today, four years after I lost my hearing after making a full recovery from Meningitis,

my boyfriend of seven years asked me the four-word question every girl wants to hear.

But I never imagined how perfect it would look as it did when he signed it to me.

"A guy and a girl can be just friends, but at one point or another, they will fall for each other... Maybe

temporarily, maybe at the wrong time, maybe too late, or maybe forever."

-Dave Matthews Band

Day 218 ☼ Date Idea   /   /

Make a Homemade Pizza Together

Most of us love pizza; now imagine creating your own designs and flavors with your loved one. Prep your own pizza and serve it during movie time!

His take on the date idea...   **Her take on the date idea...**

Day 219 ☼ Trial   /   /

What is the biggest fight you had and how did you try to resolve it?

The goal is to find out how you try to fix issues within the relationship and probably improve your attitude towards it.

His Answer...   **Her Answer...**

"I love you the way a drowning man loves air.
And it would destroy me to have you just a little."

-Rae Carson

Day 220 ☼ Jealousy   /   /

This question requires utmost honesty: Who is more jealous of you two?

Try to give a detailed example of when your partner becomes jealous. How did you fix it?

His Answer...   **Her Answer...**

Day 221 ☼ Hindrances   /   /

What keeps you holding on?

When things seem to be falling apart – you're both too busy, too occupied that you even miss dinner dates, too tired to pay attention to each other – what keeps you holding on? Create a list and read them together. This is to remind the both of you that despite the difficulties, it is your desire to be together that will always matter.

His Answer...   **Her Answer...**

"As he read, I fell in love the way you fall asleep: slowly, and then all at once."

—John Green

Day 222 ☼ Annoyance 　　　　　1 / 7 / 21

List down 5 things your partner does that irritate you.

While you may feel offended by the things you are about to discover, you may

also take the chance to improve yourself instead.

✱ Calling the Heat "HotAir"

His Answer...

1. Going on phone in the middle of a conversation.
2. Changing a song I like when we're in the car.
3. Kicking me out of the way when we're in bed. and my foot touches yours.
4. When she gets mad at me for not understanding the concept.
5. PULLING MY BEARD

Her Answer...

1. FIDGET/PLAY W/ HIS BEARD
2. TALKING DURING MOVIE
3. WHEN HE DOESN'T DO STUFF ON OUR TO-DO LIST
4. WHEN HE DOESN'T UNDERSTAND A CONCEPT I'M ALREADY OVER EXPLAINING
5. WHEN HE DOESN'T EXPLAIN HIS FEELINGS

Day 223 ☼ Disappointments 　　　　　/ 　/

How do you deal with your frustrations?

What is your biggest frustration? How are you trying to work on it?

His Answer...

Her Answer...

"When I am with you, I wish I could stop time so I could spend forever with you

and never have to leave your company."

-Megan Fleming

Day 224 ☼ Photo Prompt   /   /

See how many traveling photos you currently have. Why are you thankful for these trips and how can it be beneficial to your relationship?

"I've already been to hell and back. This time, I want to go to paradise. I want to do whatever it is you want. Because all I want is you, by my side, from this moment until forever"

-Holly Stephens

Rawr Means I Love You

Today, on our ten year wedding anniversary,

my middle school/high school sweetheart wrote me a love letter for the very first time.

The final sentence reads,

"I love you more every day, and I'm so proud to say we've been inseparable

since we were dinosaurs wrecking havoc on the playground so many moons ago."

"A part of you has grown in me, and, so you see, it's you and me, forever, and never apart; maybe in

distance but never in heart."

-Unknown

Day 225 ☼ Date Idea   /   /

Go Camping

This requires proper planning, especially if you're a first-timer. But isn't it romantic to exchange heartfelt stories over a campfire?

His take on the date idea...   **Her take on the date idea...**

Day 226 ☼ Clingy   /   /

Who do you think is clingier between the two of you?

Who acts like a child when he/she misses the other?

His Answer...   **Her Answer...**

"Love is the emblem of eternity; it confounds all notion of time:
effaces all memory of a beginning, all fear of an end."
-Madame de Stael

Day 227 ☼ Avoidance / /

Have you ever asked your partner to avoid certain people?

For instance, we may feel uncomfortable around someone who is touchy-feely, so you ask your partner to set a certain distance whenever this person is around.

His Answer...   **Her Answer...**

Day 228 ☼ Bigger World / /

(continuation)

...and is it even okay to ask your partner to choose the people he/she hangs out with, in the first place?

His Answer...   **Her Answer...**

"If the people we love are stolen from us, the way to have them live on is to never stop loving them.
Buildings burn, people die, but real love is forever."
-The Crow (1994)

Day 229 ☼ Reconciliation   /   /

What was the pettiest fight you have ever had?

Can you remember an instance which you had the pettiest fight? How did you reconcile after?

His Answer...   **Her Answer...**

Day 230 ☼ Forgiveness   /   /

How do you deal with difficult situations, say during a fight?

Do you usually give each other space, or you just can't let the day end without fixing the problem? Who usually apologizes first?

His Answer...   **Her Answer...**

"Love someone who leaves so many holes in you that if they were to walk away,
half of your soul would go with them."

-Emery Allen

Day 231 ☼ Photo Prompt   /   /

This prompt needs utmost understanding; after all, we are old enough to understand that this is just for fun: Are you brave enough to share a photo of someone you used to like so much? Say a childhood crush from school, or a teenage boy/girlfriend. Perhaps you have accidentally kept a photo in your home album. If not, you can both stalk their IG or FB profile just for the heck of it!.

"It only takes a few seconds to say goodbye to someone you love, but it will take the rest of your life to forget them, because the memory lives on forever in your heart."

-Unknown

I Want You

Today, I received this text message from my fiancé:

"I want this too. I want all of it. I want the pointless bickering, the long walks, the late night phone calls, the good morning texts. I want cute pictures with you, to hold your hand, to make food for you, to call you baby. The joking, the wrestling, the fights, the long 'how I feel' text messages on the days we aren't on the same page. I want to be one of those inseparable best friend couples that people are like 'you're still together?'
That's what I want. With you."

"There is never a time or place for true love.
It happens accidentally, in a heartbeat, in a single flashing, throbbing moment."
— Sarah Dessen

Day 232 ☼ Date Idea   /   /

Recreate Your First Date

How did your first date go? Now go back to that place and recall what exactly happened that day. Enjoy it the second time around.

His take on the date idea...   **Her take on the date idea...**

Day 233 ☼ Listener   /   /

When you have problems, who do you usually talk to for some advice?

How does a friendly advice help in calming down the situation?

His Answer...   **Her Answer...**

"You know you're in love when you can't fall asleep
because reality is finally better than your dreams."
—Dr. Seuss

Day 234 ☼ Strangers to Lovers   1 / 4 / 21

How did you feel the first time you laid eyes on your partner?

Reminisce the first time you met. Go as detailed as possible. Was there a spark, as people would say? Or was it an ordinary meeting you didn't expect would bloom into something special?

His Answer…

I was in her apartment playing with my dude Pud. She left pretty soon after I got there, but she seemed ~~chill.~~ cool. Her roommate had a huge crush on me, but I don't really like blonde girls. I didn't think it would bloom into this, but I'm so glad it did "

Her Answer…

He was in my apartment playing w/ my roommate's dog. My roommate had a crush on him. I thought he was pretty ugly but funny. JK I thought he was cute but off limits, but guess I was wrong cuz now we're in love ☺

Day 235 ☼ Decisions   / /

How do you make the decision together?

Say when you're planning to buy something. What are the things you have to consider first as a couple?

His Answer…

Her Answer…

"She was ready to deny the existence of space and time
rather than admit that love might not be eternal."
—Simone de Beauvoir

Day 236 ☼ The Past   /   /

What is your take on sharing about each other's past relationships?

Do you sometimes get into this kind of conversation, or it doesn't really matter?

His Answer...   **Her Answer...**

Day 237 ☼ Breakaway   /   /

What is the longest time that you stopped talking to each other?

How did it affect your individual lifestyle or daily routine, knowing that you are not on good terms with your loved one?

His Answer...   **Her Answer...**

"Every heart sings a song, incomplete, until another heart whispers back. Those who wish to sing always find a song. At the touch of a lover, everyone becomes a poet."

—Plato

Day 238 ☼ Photo Prompt   /   /

Go through your partner's album and pick the wackiest shot he/she got. What was his/her reaction to seeing the picture in your hands? Why do you think this shot was so funny?

"You don't love someone for their looks, or their clothes or for their fancy car,

but because they sing a song only you can hear."

—Oscar Wilde

The Truth About Nice Guys

Today, it's been five years since I was severely beaten by three bullies at a college party for stopping them from trying to bring a drugged girl home with them.

I lost a tooth, received two black eyes and severely bruised ribs from the incident, but I stopped them. This girl was my crush for three years but had never noticed me as boyfriend material until that night. When I woke up in ICU 12 hours after I was beaten up, she was sitting beside my bed, asleep while holding my hand. Since then, we've been steadily dating for five years and are engaged to be married.

Who says nice guys finish last?

"Love looks not with the eyes, but with the mind,
And therefore is winged Cupid painted blind."
—William Shakespeare

Day 239 ☼ Date Idea   /   /

Game Night with Friends

Who said dates are limited only to the two of you? Group dates can be fun if you're in the company of your good friends. Invite them over for a game night – poker, monopoly, name it!

His take on the date idea...   **Her take on the date idea...**

Day 240 ☼ Small Talks   /   /

What is your take on relationship counseling?

Do you think it is really needed, or you just need to sit and talk carefully about the issues?

His Answer...   **Her Answer...**

"Once upon a time there was a boy who loved a girl and her laughter was a question he wanted to spend his whole life answering."

—Nicole Krauss

Day 241 ☼ Full Support   /   /

How do you boost each other's confidence, especially when going through a challenging time?

How do you assure your partner that he/she is doing just fine?

His Answer...   **Her Answer...**

Day 242 ☼ Random Dates   /   /

Are dates usually difficult to decide about?

Do you have your favorite restaurant or hangout place, or you take your time in choosing?

His Answer...   **Her Answer...**

"When someone loves you, the way they say your name is different.
You know that your name is safe in their mouth."
—Jess C. Scott

Day 243 ☼ Sweetest Things   /   /

What are 3 things your partner has done this week that made you really happy?

It could be as simple as cleaning the sink without you having to ask!

His Answer...   **Her Answer...**

Day 244 ☼ On Getting Attracted   /   /

Do you think it's normal to still find other people physically attractive when you are in a relationship, especially long-term?

Let's get more serious: Again, this type of question requires utmost understanding. But keep in mind that our goal, of course, is to be more open and learn to discuss issues in a mature way. Is it enough reason to be angry with your partner? What is your take on this?

His Answer...   **Her Answer...**

"Two people in love, alone, isolated from the world, that's beautiful."

—Milan Kundera

Day 245 ☼ Photo Prompt   /   /

Showing your sentimental side to your partner once in awhile is not just normal, but also healthy for your relationship. Show him/her a picture of a beloved relative that already passed away. You may also share why you are really close to this person.

"Remember to hold hands and cherish the moment for someday t
hat person might not be there again. Give time to love, give time to speak!
And give time to share the precious thoughts in your mind."

—Bob Moorehead

Memories

Today, as my 81 year old mother and I sat in the waiting area of a restaurant,
the 1960's song "Don't Worry Baby" by The Beach Boys came on the radio,
and she started to smile.

"What are you smiling about?" I asked.

"This was our song – your dad and I, that is," she said.

"You know, your dad has been gone for almost a decade, and it's been nearly 50 years since
he and I first heard this song playing in a night club. But every time I hear it, it reminds
me of that night, dancing with him on our first official date. And that makes me smile."

"If you gave someone your heart and they died, did they take it with them?
Did you spend the rest of forever with a hole inside you that couldn't be filled?"
—Jodi Picoult

Day 246 ☼ Date Idea   /   /

The Truth or Dare Date

Prepare to perform some nasty stuff when you say "Dare" – it could be a "sexy time" for the both of you, too.

His take on the date idea...   **Her take on the date idea...**

Day 247 ☼ Advances   /   /

How do you feel when someone shows interest to your partner?

When someone is making advances to your partner, but say in a harmless way (asking for a mobile number, being extra friendly, etc), how would you handle such situation?

His Answer...   **Her Answer...**

"I loved you like a man loves a woman he never touches, only writes to,
keeps little photographs of."
—Charles Bukowski

Day 248 ☼ Irreconcilable   /   /

List down 5 relationship mistakes you consider unforgivable.

Forgive and forget that's what they say. But how about those mistakes that you
think are grave and therefore are unforgiveable?

His Answer...   **Her Answer...**

Day 249 ☼ Investments   /   /

Is it recommendable to start putting up your savings as partners?

Do you think it is practical to start putting up your savings together even when
you are not married yet, considering that you look forward to settling down in the
future?

His Answer...   **Her Answer...**

"Then I realize what it is. It's him. Something about him makes me feel like I am about to fall.
Or turn to liquid. Or burst into flames."

—Veronica Roth

Day 251 ☼ Mr. and Ms. Congeniality / /

When is being too friendly, not okay?

Sometimes, people misunderstood our welcoming attitude and interpret it as flirtatious. Do you talk about this with your partner to avoid arguments??

His Answer...   **Her Answer...**

Day 251 ☼ Hectic Schedule / /

How do you handle busy schedule?

As we get older, our responsibilities at work get all the more hectic. In times like this, how do you manage to squeeze in some quality time, in order to make sure you're just busy, but not falling apart?

His Answer...   **Her Answer...**

"Love has nothing to do with what you are expecting to get —
only with what you are expecting to give — which is everything."
—Katharine Hepburn

Day 252 ☼ Photo Prompt

Find at least 3 photos online that would best represent your current disposition in life. For example A photo of a beautifully bloomed flower, which could mean you are at the peak of your physical health. Show the photos and explain why you choose them.

"Love is friendship that has caught fire. It is quiet understanding, mutual confidence, sharing and forgiving. It is loyalty through good and bad times. It settles for less than perfection and makes allowances for human weaknesses."

-Ann Landers

Patience

Today, I waited on an elderly couple where I work. She kept forgetting things.

Turns out she has Alzheimer's disease. Her husband was so calm and understanding.

He never got annoyed having to tell her everything she had forgotten.

I witnessed true love at its best.

"Love: a wildly misunderstood although highly desirable malfunction of the heart which weakens the brain, causes eyes to sparkle, cheeks to glow, blood pressure to rise and the lips to pucker."

-Author Unknown

Day 253 ☼ Date Idea   /   /

Tech-Free Weekend

You may travel somewhere near or simply cuddle at home; the main goal is to be away from any gadgets and the internet for the entire weekend – you'll be surprised at how more intimate your weekend can be!

His take on the date idea...   **Her take on the date idea...**

Day 254 ☼ Being Away   /   /

What is your take on group or company travels without your presence?

Do you trust your parent enough to let him/her travel far and be away with people you don't know for a few days?

His Answer...   **Her Answer...**

"A loving heart is the truest wisdom."

-Charles Dickens

Day 255 ☼ Intimacy / /

How do you show your romantic love to your partner in a more intimate manner?

On being intimate: Without your partner having to ask, how do you know that he/she wants to make love?

His Answer...   **Her Answer...**

Day 256 ☼ Dealing with an Ex / /

Is it okay to be friends with an ex-boy/girlfriend?

What is your opinion about being friends (or at least being socially connected) with an ex-boy/girlfriend? Are you comfortable knowing that your partner's ex, hangs out with the same set of friends?

His Answer...   **Her Answer...**

"Absence is to love as wind is to fire; it extinguishes the small and enkindles the great."

-Comte de Bussy-Rabutin

Day 257 ☼ Cheating   /   /

Why do others cheat?

Without putting your personal situation in the picture, why do think some people cheat? Is it a behavioral problem or the partner's effort isn't really enough to make the other one satisfied?

His Answer...   **Her Answer...**

Day 258 ☼ Dishonesty   /   /

What are the simple actions that can be considered as cheating?

What is your definition of cheating? See if you can explain in detail.

His Answer...   **Her Answer...**

"Absence makes the heart grow fonder."

-Thomas Haynes Bayly

Day 259 ☼ Photo Prompt   /   /

What is one photo that would best describe the kind of love you have for your partner? Try to explain in details.

"Love is a force more formidable than any other. It is invisible - it cannot be seen or measured,

yet it is powerful enough to transform you in a moment,

and offer you more joy than any material possession could."

-Barbara De Angelis

When the Wait is Worth It

Today, he's driving to my college apartment to spend my last week of school with me. This will be the first night of the rest of our lives. After 3 years dating long distance, a 12 month deployment to Iraq, and the rest of the time spent 3 states apart due to his serving in the Army, we are finally going to be together, permanently, in one place. Waiting this long for each other, and finally getting to start our life TOGETHER makes me happy.

"Love is a fabric which never fades,
no matter how often it is washed in the water of adversity and grief."
-Robert Fulghum

Day 260 ☼ Date Idea   /   /

Build a Fort

If you're not really into camping outside, then you can simply build a blanket fort indoors! Fill it with lots of pillows and play a nice music while you enjoy the rest of the night.

His take on the date idea...   **Her take on the date idea...**

Day 261 ☼ The One   /   /

How do you say that you found the right one?

What are the factors you consider before acknowledging that you have finally found the right person to settle down with?

His Answer...   **Her Answer...**

"Love is often the fruit of marriage."

-French (on marriage)

Day 262 ☼ Helping Hand   /   /

What do you think of sharing chores as a couple?

Do you think women are really bound to focus on housework, while men should merely focus on working?

His Answer...   **Her Answer...**

Day 263 ☼ Make Love   /   /

How much sex do you think is normal?

Is it once a day or once a week, perhaps? The goal is to be aware of your partner's needs, at the same acknowledging when it is seldom, too much, or basically just enough.

His Answer...   **Her Answer...**

"Love will find a way."

-Unknown

Day 264 ☼ Being Comfy / /

How comfortable you both are with each other.

Do you mind if your partner walks into the bathroom while you are still using it?

His Answer...   Her Answer...

Day 265 ☼ Shared Privacy / /

Is it okay to have "shared privacy"?

What is your take on "shared privacy"? – sharing things, sharing a bathroom, sharing social media accounts. Is it okay especially when you're committed long-term?

His Answer...   Her Answer...

"Not all who make love, make marriages."

-Russian (on marriage)

Day 266 ☼ Photo Prompt   /   /

Show your partner a photo that would illustrate the kind of childhood you had. If you were a playful kid back then, perhaps a photo of a children-filled playground will do. It's up to you.

"One who marries for love alone will have bad days but good nights."

-Egyptian (on marriage)

Falling For You Again

Today my Ex husband asked me to marry him, I said yes.

We were married when I was 19, divorced later on and then our lives somehow lead our hearts back together. We are going to be married in 2 weeks, on what could have been our 16th wedding anniversary. Our children cried with joy when we told them today.

"Parting is such sweet sorrow."

-William Shakespeare

Day 267 ☼ Date Idea   /   /

Try Yoga

Especially for those couples who are always busy working; try yoga and practice the art of proper breathing together!

His take on the date idea...   **Her take on the date idea...**

Day 268 ☼ Married Life   /   /

What kind of married life do you wish to have?

List your ideal married life you wish to have.

His Answer...   **Her Answer...**

"You can't buy love."

-Unknown

Day 269 ☼ Obstacles   /   /

What is one thing you consider as an ultimate relationship breaker?

Discuss this in detail and see how you two are trying to work on your differences to make the relationship work.

His Answer...   **Her Answer...**

Day 270 ☼ Dominance   /   /

Who is more dominant in your relationship?

Without being offended, who do you think is more dominant between the two of you? How do you define "dominance" within your relationship?

His Answer...   **Her Answer...**

"Love isn't something you find. Love is something that finds you."

-Loretta Young

Day 271 ☼ Two in One   /   /

Is your partner your best friend?

When it comes to your personal sentiments, do you confide more with your partner or someone else (say, your best friend)?

His Answer...   **Her Answer...**

Day 272 ☼ Handling Differences   /   /

How do you handle the differences between you and your partner's (religious and social) beliefs?

Was this ever an issue or is it something that you guys aren't bothered about?

His Answer...   **Her Answer...**

"Sometimes the heart sees what is invisible to the eye."

-H. Jackson Brown, Jr.

Day 273 ☼ Photo Prompt   /   /

Choose two photos that will describe your personality: The serious and the funny side. Try to go into detail as to why you choose the following. It will be interesting to hear how you view your own character.

"Love is when the other person's happiness is more important than your own."

-H. Jackson Brown, Jr.

Listen

Sometimes we show our love when we are quiet and do not say a word,

at the other times – we speak loud to express it. Sometimes we show our love by

impulsiveness. Many times we have to show our love when we forgive someone.

The problem with our world is that people don't learn to listen to each other.

They hear the words, but they don't listen to the actions that accompany the words and do

not mind the expression on the face. We have to listen to see love in and around us.

If we listen attentively we will reveal that we are a lot more loved than we realize;

we will find out that the world is a place full of love.

"Love doesn't make the world go 'round. Love is what makes the ride worthwhile."

-Franklin P. Jones

Day 274 ☼ Date Idea   / /

Ballroom Night

Sway your body to classical Cha Cha, Samba or Rumba! It's also a chance to dress up nicely!

His take on the date idea...   **Her take on the date idea...**

Day 275 ☼ Settling Issues   / /

Should religion be an issue when two people wanted to be together?

What is your take on differences in religious practices and beliefs?

His Answer...   **Her Answer...**

"Love is composed of a single soul inhabiting two bodies."

-Aristotle

Day 276 ☼ Involvement   /   /

What exactly would you do if you learn that a common friend was cheating on his/her spouse?

Do you think the partner should know about it, or would you rather not get involved?

His Answer...   **Her Answer...**

Day 277 ☼ Anxiety   /   /

What are the things you were worried about the time you just started dating?

Were you worried that he/she might be just playing around? Or were you not ready to be committed to a serious relationship back then?

His Answer...   **Her Answer...**

"Love is a fruit in season at all times, and within reach of every hand."

-Mother Teresa

Day 278 ☼ Expectations / /

How much are you willing to give up just to meet your partner's expectations?

For instance, are you ready to let go of the job you really love doing or do you think there is another way to settle things out?

His Answer...   **Her Answer...**

Day 279 ☼ Disappointments / /

When was the last time your partner disappointed you?

What was it about? How did you try to resolve the issue?

His Answer...   **Her Answer...**

"Love is a canvas furnished by Nature and embroidered by imagination."

-Voltaire

Day 280 ☼ Photo Prompt / /

Find a photo that will illustrate the kind of life you want to enjoy when you become older. Is it a house on the beachside? Or a garden filled with your favorite flowers? It's normal to look forward to getting older together when you are so much in love; try to imagine how you'd like to spend your golden years together.

"The best and most beautiful things in the world cannot be seen nor even touched, but just felt in the heart."

-Anne Sullivan

When You are Missing Someone

Whenever we are apart, I am constantly thinking of you. It is crazy how every little thing can remind me of you. Your smile, your laugh, and the sound of your voice are never far from my thoughts. I can remember the touch of your hand as though you are right here sitting next to me. No matter how far apart we are, you are always in my heart and in my thoughts, and your name is always on the edge of my lips. Your presence in a room makes my light feel so much lighter and my heart yearns for you when you are far away from me.

Now that we are miles apart, I cannot wait until we are together again.

When I see you again, I will never want to leave your side.

"In the arithmetic of love, one plus one equals everything, and two minus one equals nothing."

-Mignon McLaughlin

Day 281 ☼ Date Idea   /   /

Set Up a Small Home Garden

Gardening can be therapeutic. Ask your partner to help you clean up the soil and plant some nice flowers that can make your home a lot more beautiful.

His take on the date idea...   **Her take on the date idea...**

Day 282 ☼ First Meeting   /   /

What did you first notice when you saw your partner for the first time?

Let's reminisce: What was the first thing that attracted you most about your partner during your first few meetings? Does he/she still carry the same personality?

His Answer...   **Her Answer...**

"Love is a great beautifier."

-Louisa May Alcott

Day 283 ☼ Getting Stronger / /

How do you maintain a strong relationship?

These are some of the factors in maintaining a strong relationship: Sexual satisfaction, maintaining the friendship, honesty and being open about your feelings. Now organize the following based on its importance and explain each of them.

His Answer...   **Her Answer...**

Day 284 ☼ Confirmations / /

When and how did you know that you love your partner?

How did you admit it for the first time? Was it an easy journey or you went through some difficult times before you commit to an exclusive relationship?

His Answer...   **Her Answer...**

"To be your friend was all I ever wanted; to be your lover was all I ever dreamed."

–Valerie Lombardo

Day 285 ☼ Behavior   /   /

What are your partner's best and worst qualities?

Write down two things: Your partner's best and worst qualities. Explain your reasons for your answer. Again, be cool about it and you'll be surprised at how positively it will affect your relationship.

His Answer...   **Her Answer...**

Day 286 ☼ Being Open   /   /

Do you feel comfortable sharing your insights?

Are you the type of person who always shares what you think or feels with your partner? Or do you prefer keeping things to yourself? How much 'sharing' do you think is healthy and how much is not?

His Answer...   **Her Answer...**

"My love for you has no depth, its boundaries are ever-expanding."

–Christina White

Day 287 ☼ Photo Prompt   /   /

If you were to describe your career life at the moment, what photo would you use?

"I seem to have loved you in numberless forms, numberless times, in life after life,

in age after age forever."

–Rabindranath Tagore

How Special They Are

You are such a special person. When I think about the fact that you are in my life,
I truly cannot believe how lucky I am to have found you.

You are so caring, loving, and thoughtful. I know that I couldn't have found a better
person than you to live my life with. You are truly one of a kind, a diamond in the rough, a
golden ticket that I am lucky to have won. I am so lucky and so grateful that you chose me.

"I love you without knowing how, or when, or from where. I love you simply,
without problems or pride."
–Pablo Neruda

Day 288 ☼ Date Idea   /   /

Play in the Rain

Instead of staying indoors during a rainy day, try to make the best of the situation by going out and enjoying the gloomy weather! Play and run like little kids and you'll be surprised at how refreshing it is to simply enjoy what nature has to offer.

His take on the date idea...   **Her take on the date idea...**

Day 289 ☼ Confidentiality   /   /

How good are you at keeping secrets?

Let's be honest: When someone shares a secret to you, do you really keep it to yourself, or do you actually share it with your partner, considering that you trust him/her enough?

His Answer...   **Her Answer...**

"You're nothing short of my everything."

–Ralph Block

Day 290 ☼ View Point   /   /

Do you and your partner share the same philosophy in life?

How does it affect your relationship in general?

His Answer...   **Her Answer...**

Day 291 ☼ Objectives   /   /

List down 3 to 5 things that you wish your partner would do more.

The goal is to let them know about their shortcomings without starting an argument.

His Answer...   **Her Answer...**

"My heart is and always will be yours."

–Jane Austen

Day 292 ☼ Present Status   /   /

How do you define your current relationship status?

Are you guys still in the process of knowing each other? Or do you think you've

known each other long enough to actually start making plans for your future?

His Answer...   **Her Answer...**

Day 293 ☼ Assurance   /   /

How to you handle jealousy?

Jealousy and insecurities are normal, granting that they do not really affect your

life as a whole. But how do you reassure your partner that he/she is good enough?

His Answer...   **Her Answer...**

"Your love shines in my heart as sun that shines upon the earth."

–Eleanor Di Guillo

Day 294 ☼ Photo Prompt

Collect a few photos of home appliances or gadgets you'd like to invest in the future. This could be a fun way to plan how you'd like your dream house to look like. A laundry machine? A big comfy sofa? Or a king-sized bed? You tell us!

"If I had to choose between breathing and loving you
I would use my last breath to tell you I love you."
–DeAnna Anderson

Growing Old Together

There are so many people out there in the world, but you are the one person in the entire universe that I can imagine happily growing old with. No matter how much time passes by or how old we get, no matter how many gray hairs and wrinkles we both end up getting, I know that you are the one person in the world that I am truly meant to grow old with.

I love you so much for who you are and I could never get tired of you, even on the days where we have our disagreements. As long as we are side by side and hand in hand, I can grow old knowing that I am the luckiest person in the world because I will have you right next to me.

"You're always the first and the last thing on this heart of mine. No matter where I go, or what I do, I'm thinking of you."
–Dierks Bentley

Day 295 ☼ Date Idea   /   /

Ride a Bicycle

If you're not up for a jog, then cycling may be a good alternative. Cycle early in the morning and wait for the sunset along the road.

His take on the date idea...   **Her take on the date idea...**

Day 296 ☼ Resentment   /   /

How far does your anger lead you to?

Ladies, I want to hear you out: Have you ever been so angry that you had to slap your partner? Tell us a bit more.

His Answer...   **Her Answer...**

"My love for you is past the mind, beyond my heart, and into my soul."

–Boris Kodjoe

Day 297 ☼ Planning   /   /

Are you good at planning?

Are you the kind of couple who takes time in carefully planning an activity, or do you enjoy spontaneity? What are the pros and cons?

His Answer...   **Her Answer...**

Day 298 ☼ Privacy   /   /

How do you feel about the use of social media when you are committed to a serious relationship?

Should you know your partner's password and be updated with his online activities? Or do you think it is part of his/her personal privacy that you should not bother about?

His Answer...   **Her Answer...**

"In short I will part with anything for you, but you."

–Mary Wortley Montagu

Day 299 ☼ Being Too Friendly   /   /

Is it okay to be friendly?

Is it okay when your partner communicates with a friend from the opposite sex, in a really amiable way, but regularly? What is your take on this?

His Answer...   **Her Answer...**

Day 300 ☼ Distance and Time   /   /

Is it okay to have long distance relationship?

How would you react if your partner was offered a really good job that requires him/her to travel and be away from you most of the time?

His Answer...   **Her Answer...**

"Each day I love you more, today more than yesterday and less than tomorrow."

–Rosemonde Gerard

Day 301 ☼ Photo Prompt   /   /

Find a photo of one particular thing that always reminds you of your partner. Hand it to him/her without explaining first. Let your partner guess why you chose the picture. Whether your partner got it wrong or right, let him/her hear your reason.

"I don't wanna close my eyes, I don't wanna fall asleep,
cuz I'd miss you babe and I don't wanna miss a thing."
–Aerosmith

A Special Love

Our love is something that is truly special and there is no other love like ours in the world.

I feel as if I have won the lottery with you, someone who is so special and magical,

who makes my life and my world a thousand times better just by being there.

When I look at you, I know that I have truly hit the jackpot. All you have to do in order to

warm my heart is be the loving, caring person that you are.

Together, we can do so much and help each other realize our dreams

because we truly have a love that is special.

"Love understands love; it needs no talk."

–Francis Havergal

Day 302 ☼ Date Idea   /   /

Reminisce at the Rooftop

Yep, climb up in there and lie next to each other while looking back at all the years you've spent together. Stargaze and plan your future.

His take on the date idea...   **Her take on the date idea...**

Day 303 ☼ On Being Strict   /   /

Are there any personal reminders that you need to strictly follow all the time?
Do you usually have personal reminders whenever your partner is going out without you – like to be careful with what she wears, for instance, or to avoid speaking with other women? Try to explain in detail.

His Answer...   **Her Answer...**

"Love stretches your heart and makes you big inside."

–Margaret Walker

Day 304 ☼ Courtship   /   /

What do you consider the most memorable part of your courtship days?

Reminisce this phase and rekindle the spark you felt when you were just starting out.

His Answer...   **Her Answer...**

Day 305 ☼ Excitement   /   /

Do you really think relationships become less and less exciting as it gets longer?

They say some couples become too comfortable that they stop exerting effort to please each other. What is your take on this?

His Answer...   **Her Answer...**

"Love brings to life whatever is dead around us."

–Franz Rosenzweig

Day 306 ☼ Affection in Public   /   /

What is your take on displaying your affection in public places?

How much do you think is okay, and how much is actually too much?

His Answer...   **Her Answer...**

Day 307 ☼ Being Hit On   /   /

How exactly would you like your partner to react if he/she is being hit on?

How do you try to react on instances like this? Try to put more details on this.

His Answer...   **Her Answer...**

"In your smile I see something more beautiful than the stars."

–Beth Revis

Day 308 ☼ Photo Prompt　　　　　　　　　/　　/

Let us see how much you know your partner: Collect three photos that will each show the things he/she loves. Show them one by one and let your partner decide whether you got it right, or not.

"It was a million tiny little things that, when you added them all up,

they meant we were supposed to be together... and I knew it."

–Tom Hanks

A Perfect Match

Whether it is mere fate or coincidence that brought us together, it does not really matter. All I know is that we were meant to be together forever. I am made for you and you are made for me. We are a perfect match and we complement each other so well.

We always bring out the best in each other and I know that even though there are billions of people in the world, I know without a doubt in my mind that you are the only person in the world for me. We are a match made in heaven and a perfect match here on Earth.

"I saw that you were perfect, and so I loved you.
Then I saw that you were not perfect and I loved you even more"
–Angelita Lim

Day 309 ☼ Date Idea   /   /

Drink and Strip

Prepare some beer and drink with your partner while playing a card game. One will have to strip for every time he/she losses.

His take on the date idea...   **Her take on the date idea...**

Day 310 ☼ Road to Forever   /   /

In your own words and experience, what is the secret of a successful relationship?

List down 5 of them and try to explain each.

His Answer...   **Her Answer...**

"You are my heart, my life, my entire existence."

–Julie Kagawa

Day 311 ☼ Personal Space   /   /

Are you open to having a personal space for some time?

Do you still try to catch up with each other before the day ends, or do you prefer to maximize your rest time and just try to talk about your days off?

His Answer...   **Her Answer...**

Day 312 ☼ Update   /   /

(Continuation)

...and how important is it to regularly update each other despite being very busy at work? What could happen if you let the weeks just pass by without asking how he/she's doing?

His Answer...   **Her Answer...**

"I swear I couldn't love you more than I do right now, and yet I know I will tomorrow"

–Leo C hristopher

Day 313 ☼ A Love to Last   /   /

How do you try to work on these to keep your relationship worry-free and healthy?

List down 5 detrimental factors that can ruin a relationship; it could be a habit or a behavior.

His Answer...   **Her Answer...**

Day 314 ☼ Jealousy is Unhealthy   /   /

How much jealousy is actually unhealthy?

This is a very important issue to address in every relationship, so try to expound on this.

His Answer...   **Her Answer...**

"Whatever our souls are made of, his and mine are the same."
–Emily Brontë

Day 315 ☼ Photo Prompt   /   /

A smart game to test each other's memory: Pick 3 photos that have significance in your relationship. It could be a direct remembrance or just a hint. The goal is to test how vivid your partner's memory is when it comes to things or events that are both memorable to you.

"There is always some madness in love. But there is also always some reason in madness."
–Friedrich Nietzsche

A Special Feeling

When I look at you, I always feel so much stronger and surer of myself.

When I think about you, I feel so happy knowing that there is someone out there

in the world who loves me as much as I love them. You always make me

feel like anything in this world is possible.

With your love, it really does feel like I can do anything that I set my mind to.

Your love is a miracle that I am so happy to have received. Being with you is a special

feeling that I never want to lose. Knowing you and having you in my life has filled me with

so much hope and a deeper sense of appreciation for everything that I have in my life.

Because of you, I feel special and I know that what we have together is special.

"Being deeply loved by someone gives you strength,

while loving someone deeply gives you courage."

–Lao Tzu

Day 316 ☼ Date Idea   /   /

Create a Scrapbook

This can be a fun way to rekindle the spark. Collect some photos of you together
and put it in a book with fun captions. Reminisce the good times through each
photo and realize once again how much you love each other.

His take on the date idea...   **Her take on the date idea...**

Day 317 ☼ Pleasure   /   /

What excites you?

Enumerate the simple things your partner does that actually (or accidentally) turn
you on.

His Answer...   **Her Answer...**

"Love doesn't make the world go 'round. Love is what makes the ride worthwhile."

–Franklin P. Jones

Day 318 ☼ Showing Respect   /   /

What kind of behavior or action makes you feel respected?

It could be a simple gesture, like allowing you to choose whether you'd like to spend some intimate time or to rest first when you are really tired.

His Answer...   **Her Answer...**

Day 319 ☼ Having Other One   /   /

What is your take on having a best friend from the opposite sex?

Some partners are okay with this while others are just not comfortable. How about you?

His Answer...   **Her Answer...**

"As soon go kindle fire with snow, as seek to quench the fire of love with words."

–Shakespeare

Day 320 ☼ Expression of Love   /   /

Other than being vocal about it, in what other ways can you actually express your love?

There are lots of ways to express your love to your partner. List at least 5 ways on how you show your love to him or her.

His Answer...   **Her Answer...**

Day 321 ☼ Strength in Crying   /   /

How would you feel if you see him crying?

On breaking the norms: Do you think it is okay for men to cry, especially when they are going through a difficult time?

His Answer...   **Her Answer...**

"If you wish to be loved, show more of your faults than your virtues."

–Edward G. Bulwer-Lytton

Day 322 ☼ Photo Prompt   /   /

Find a photo that best describes your partner's characteristic. For instance, a picture of a roller coaster may describe your partner's mood swings. Be creative in choosing.

"Love is an irresistible desire to be irresistibly desired."

–Robert Frost

A Strong Bond

What we have together is unique. It is a special bond that is strong and unbreakable.
We can make it through anything we encounter and we only grow stronger
from the trials we face together. Together, we are strong.
Being with you has made me a better person and I can't believe that I found you.

Ever since I met you, I never want to let you go.
The attraction that you and I share is one that is so intense and I never want to be
separated from you.

"A kiss is a lovely trick designed by nature to stop speech when words become superfluous."
–Ingrid Bergman

Day 323 ☼ Date Idea / /

Drink in the Tub

If you don't have the time and budget for that most-awaited spa date, you can simply set up your own bathroom by creating a romantic ambiance. Use a dim light, put some rose petals in the floor and light a scented candle. Have a bubble bath together – but don't forget to play romantic music as you enjoy sipping your wine (or beer, really up to you).

His take on the date idea...   **Her take on the date idea...**

Day 324 ☼ Playlist / /

Listen to Each Other's Playlist

Make a playlist of all the songs that remind you of your partner. Let him/her listen to it afterward.

His Answer...   **Her Answer...**

"Love is the wisdom of the fool and the folly of the wise."

–Samuel Johnson

Day 325 ☼ Desires   /   /

Are you open to expressing your emotional and physical desires?

Are you too shy to even open this up to your partner? Why do you think being transparent about our needs is an important factor in any relationship?

His Answer...   **Her Answer...**

Day 326 ☼ Being Independent   /   /

In what way do you prefer to be supported or encouraged?

Do you prefer to be allowed to decide on your own, or do you appreciate personal advice?

His Answer...   **Her Answer...**

"He's more myself than I am."

–Emily Bronte

Day 327 ☼ Gratification / /

In what way do you try to please your partner?

Some women exert effort in dressing up nicely or putting on something sexy; some men try to be more thoughtful of their partner's needs. What about you?

His Answer...   **Her Answer...**

Day 328 ☼ Dealing with In-Laws / /

How do you maintain a harmonious relationship with your future in-laws?

How important is it to build and maintain a good relationship with your partner's family, especially if you are looking forward to hopefully settle down in the future?

His Answer...   **Her Answer...**

"The most powerful weapon on earth is the human soul on fire."

–Ferdinand Foch

Day 329 ☼ Photo Prompt   /   /

Tell your partner how you feel about him/her, in general, using only 3 photos. For instance, you may show a photo of a beachside hut (expressing peacefulness) to tell how at peace you are when he/she is around. Go figure!

"Love is when he gives you a piece of your soul, that you never knew was missing."

–Torquato Tasso

Always There For You

I hope that you know that I will always be there for you. Not just for the good times when we are celebrating and enjoying life, but for the bad times as well.

When you are sad, stressed out, or angry, just know that I will be by your side to see you through the tough times. I will hold your hand and lead you through the storm. And when things are going great, I will be there to cheer you on and dance with you..

"I love that feeling of being in love, the effect of having butterflies when you wake up in the morning. That is special."
-Jennifer Aniston

Day 330 ☼ Date Idea   /   /

Breakfast Date in Bed

Start your day right by prepping a nice meal you can share in bed. Cook your favorite breakfast if possible.

His take on the date idea...   **Her take on the date idea...**

Day 331 ☼ One Direction   /   /

How do you keep things in the right path?

Based on your own experience of being in a serious relationship, what 3 pieces of advice can you give other people on how to keep things working?

His Answer...   **Her Answer...**

"Love is the flower you've got to let grow."

–John Lennon

Day 332 ☼ Growing Old   /   /

How would you like to spend quality time as both of you become a lot older?

Would you like to travel as much as you can, or would you like your daily life to be more calm and peaceful?

His Answer...   **Her Answer...**

Day 333 ☼ Ultimate Vision   /   /

What is your ultimate dream as a couple?

Others dream of traveling to Paris to see the Eiffel Tower. Some couples want to climb up a mountain's summit together. What about you two?

His Answer...   **Her Answer...**

"The hunger for love is much more difficult to remove than the hunger for bread."

–Mother Teresa

Day 334 ☼ Dream Date   /   /

Is your partner the exact type of person you dreamed of dating?

Did you actually 'break' your own standard because you really felt the connection between the two of you?

His Answer...   **Her Answer...**

Day 335 ☼ De-stressing   /   /

What can your partner do to make you feel better after a long, stressful day?

Will a head massage do? Or do you prefer an intimate talk over a cup of coffee?

His Answer...   **Her Answer...**

"A woman knows the face of the man she loves as a sailor knows the open sea."

–Honore de Balzac

Day 336 ☼ Photo Prompt   /   /

Express your desire to have a family through photos. Do you want to have a big family or just a small one? In what kind of environment do you want your future kids to grow up? This may be a way to discuss the possibility of having a family without feeling awkward towards each other.

"Love knows not distance; it hath no continent; its eyes are for the stars."

–Gilbert Parker

An Adventure

Knowing you has been such an amazing adventure. Ever since I met you,

I knew that my life would never ever be the same again. Since I have known you,

life has never been sweeter. Thanks to you, my life is more exciting and full of happiness.

You have helped me open so many doors that I would have left closed and undiscovered if it

were not for you. With you, I am bolder, less afraid, and ready to conquer my next

adventure. Knowing you, loving you, and being loved by you in return has been the best

adventure of my life and I never want our adventure to come to an end.

"Love does not begin and end the way we seem to think it does.

Love is a battle, love is a war; love is a growing up."

–James A. Baldwin

Day 337 ☼ Date Idea   /   /

Streetfood and Night Walk

If you're still up late at night, it's probably a good time to go for a night walk and find some street foods you can both munch into!

His take on the date idea...   **Her take on the date idea...**

Day 338 ☼ The Big Rock   /   /

What was the most painful thing your partner has gone through?

What did you do to comfort him/her amidst everything?

His Answer...   **Her Answer...**

"The art of love is largely the art of persistence."

–Albert Ellis

Day 339 ☼ Ideal Partner   /   /

Prior to meeting your partner, what exactly was your ideal man/woman?

List down the qualities of your ideal man or woman.

His Answer...   **Her Answer...**

Day 340 ☼ Witty Partner   /   /

Are you attracted to a person with good sense of humor?

Many people believe that being funny adds up to someone's overall attractiveness.

Do you agree or disagree?

His Answer...   **Her Answer...**

"There is no remedy for love but to love more."

–Henry David Thoreau

Day 341 ☼ A Good Influence   /   /

Is your partner a good influence to your overall well-being?

What particular traits or beliefs have you acquired through your partner's influence (and vice versa)?

His Answer...   **Her Answer...**

Day 342 ☼ Advancement   /   /

How do you handle advancement from others?

Considering that your partner is responsible enough not to entertain any form of advancement from others, how do you feel knowing that there are people who are physically attracted to him/her? Does it make you feel threatened, or does it make you feel prouder than ever?

His Answer...   **Her Answer...**

"If you find someone you love in your life, then hang on to that love."

–Princess Diana

Day 343 ☼ Photo Prompt   /   /

Show a photo of your dream country. Share how you are planning to make that dream come true.

"Love does not consist in gazing at each other,
but in looking outward together in the same direction."
–Antoine de Saint-Exupery

The Person of My Dreams

I always thought I knew who the man / woman of my dreams was until I met you.

Any thoughts I could have of the perfect person went out the window when you came into

my life. You have exceeded all of my expectations. Even with your flaws you are perfect

because you are the perfect person for me. I could not have dreamed up a better person.

Being with you is like being in a dream that I never want to wake up from.

"Love is of all passions the strongest,

for it attacks simultaneously the head, the heart and the senses."

–Lao Tzu

Day 344 ☼ Date Idea   /   /

Rollerskate Together

Coz, of course, nothing beats the old school! Go to the nearest park and enjoy roller-skating like the silly kids you once were.

His take on the date idea...   **Her take on the date idea...**

Day 345 ☼ Being Sexy   /   /

Do you consider yourself sexy?

What is your definition of being sexy?

His Answer...   **Her Answer...**

"Touch seems to be as essential as sunlight."

–Diane Ackerman

Day 346 ☼ Secrets   /   /

Do you know your partner 101%?

How well do you know your partner? Do you know your partner's darkest and deepest secrets?

His Answer...   **Her Answer...**

Day 347 ☼ Favorite Dish   /   /

What is his/her favorite restaurant, along with the meal that he/she usually orders?

List the top 3 favorite dishes that your partner likes to eat?

His Answer...   **Her Answer...**

"I like not only to be loved, but also to be told I am loved."

–George Eliot

Day 348 ☼ Best Points   /   /

What are your partner's strengths?

Tell us about 3 things that your partner is actually good at.

His Answer...   **Her Answer...**

Day 349 ☼ Worst Points   /   /

(Continuation)

... and 3 more things that your partner is actually bad at.

His Answer...   **Her Answer...**

"The first duty of love is to listen."

– Paul Tillich

Day 350 ☼ Photo Prompt   / /

Choose 3 photos of nature or natural events to represent your current state of mind. For instance, if you are going through some personal dilemma at the moment, then you may choose a photo of a destructive typhoon. The goal is to help your partner fully understand what is running through your mind.

"We can only learn to love by loving."
–Iris Murdoch

When You Are Long Distance

Being in a long distance relationship is not easy by any means, but I would not trade this relationship with anything in the world. Nothing in my life is worth more than you, even when you are far away from me. Even though we are separated by many, many miles, my heart has never felt closer to anyone else's heart but yours. Even when we are so far apart, I feel closer to you now more than ever.

I can't wait to see you, but no matter how far apart we are from one another, I always cherish having you in my life, no matter what the distance between us is. I constantly look forward to the moment when we are reunited once again.

"There can be no deep disappointment where there is not deep love."
–Martin Luther King, Jr.

Day 351 ☼ Date Idea   /   /

Booksale Date

This only applies to the couples who both love to read. Nothing beats the feeling of finding a cheap book in a book sale!

His take on the date idea...   **Her take on the date idea...**

Day 352 ☼ Just Emotions   /   /

What is one movie that made him/her cry or become emotional?

List down the most memorable line or scenario from that movie.

His Answer...   **Her Answer...**

"Love is not only something you feel, it is something you do."

–David Wilkerson

Day 353 ☼ Dislikes   /   /

What is one thing he/she hates doing? (Working out, waking up early, etc)

How do you encourage your partner to do those unwanted routines?

His Answer...   **Her Answer...**

Day 354 ☼ Attraction   /   /

How do you handle situations when someone shows interest on you?

Do you tell that to your partner? Or do you keep that to yourself?

His Answer...   **Her Answer...**

"When we are in love we seem to ourselves quite different from what we were before."

–Blaise Pascal

Day 355 ☼ Personal Time   / /

Do you value a "me time"?

Do you prefer staying close to your partner most of the time? Or do you want to spend quality time alone for some time?

His Answer...   **Her Answer...**

Day 356 ☼ Indifference   / /

How do you handle indifferences?

Were there instances that misunderstandings occur due to your indifferences? How do you manage to avoid incidents like that?

His Answer...   **Her Answer...**

"For small creatures such as we the vastness is bearable only through love."

–Carl Sagan

Day 357 ☼ Photo Prompt

One photo to describe your personality; it could be anything – perhaps a cartoon character to emphasize your childish side or a bookshelf to express your love for knowledge.

"Only divine love bestows the keys of knowledge."

–Arthur Rimbaud

Showing How Much You Love Them

I can only use so many words in the dictionary to show you how much I love you.

I love you so much that you are always on my mind, putting a smile on my face and making my heart skip a beat. There are so many ways for me to express my love and I plan on showing you just how much love I have for you for the rest of my life. I hope that my actions let you know the extent of my affection, adoration, and commitment to you.

"A part of kindness consists in loving people more than they deserve."

–Joseph Joubert

Day 358 ☼ Date Idea   /   /

Game Night with Friends

Who said dates are limited only to the two of you? Group dates can be fun if you're in the company of your good friends. Invite them over for a game night – poker, monopoly, name it!

His take on the date idea...   **Her take on the date idea...**

Day 359 ☼ Being Unloved   /   /

When was the last time you feel unloved?

What was it about? How did you try to resolve the issue?

His Answer...   **Her Answer...**

"Love is the attempt to form a friendship inspired by beauty."

–Marcus Tullius Cicero

Day 360 ☼ First Glance   /   /

Do you believe in love at first sight?

Reminisce the moment when you first saw your boy/girlfriend. Was it magical?
Or was it just one of the ordinary meetings that you've had? Was it a love at first
sight?

His Answer...   **Her Answer...**

Day 361 ☼ Marry Me   /   /

Were there any plans of settling down?

During coffee dates or movie night, were there any conversations about marrying
and settling down? Do you already have plans?

His Answer...   **Her Answer...**

"The inner reality of love can be recognized only by love."
–Hans Urs von Balthasar

Day 362 ☼ Privacy   /   /

Do you check your partner's phone?

Use of phones and social media accounts is considered private. No one is excused even for married couples. However, it is still okay if with permission. What is your take on this?

His Answer...   **Her Answer...**

Day 363 ☼ Far From You   /   /

Is it okay to be away from the person you loved the most?

How would you react if your partner decides to transfer to other country because of a family decision that requires him/her to be away from you?

His Answer...   **Her Answer...**

"Love is energy of life."

–Robert Browning

Day 364 ☼ Relationship Goals   /   /

What are your goals for the next year?

The year is about to end. You were able to accomplish many goals this year and you might be considering of listing down your bucket list for next year. List down top 5 things that you want to accomplish for the next year.

His Answer...

Her Answer...

"The ear is the avenue to the heart."

–Voltaire

Day 365 ☼ Photo Prompt   /   /

The year is almost over. Share a photo of your most unforgettable moment. Recall that time and reminisce the love that you shared for 365 days. Keep the love burning!

"Stolen kisses are always sweetest."

–Leigh Hunt

How Much You Need Them

I hope you know how much you mean to me. You are such an important part of my life.

In fact, you are the center of my life. Everything I do is for us and I hope you know that I

am always trying to do the right thing that will make our relationship a stronger one.

You have inspired me to be the best version of myself that I can possibly be and I hope that I

can somehow repay you for everything that you have done for me.

Without you, I would be a completely different person.

You have taught me so much about life and because of you, I truly know what love is.

"Love can be unselfish, in the sense of being benevolent and generous, without being selfless."

–Mortimer Adler

Made in the USA
Coppell, TX
21 December 2020